James Jackson Jarves

**Old masters**

the history of painting from A.D. 1200 to the best periods of Italian art

James Jackson Jarves

**Old masters**
*the history of painting from A.D. 1200 to the best periods of Italian art*

ISBN/EAN: 9783742860538

Manufactured in Europe, USA, Canada, Australia, Japa

Cover: Foto ©Thomas Meinert / pixelio.de

Manufactured and distributed by brebook publishing software
(www.brebook.com)

James Jackson Jarves

# Old masters

# DESCRIPTIVE CATALOGUE

OF

# "OLD MASTERS,"

## COLLECTED BY JAMES J. JARVES,

TO ILLUSTRATE

### The History of Painting

FROM A.D. 1200 TO THE BEST PERIODS OF ITALIAN ART,

AND

DEPOSITED IN THE "INSTITUTE OF FINE ARTS,"

636, BROADWAY, NEW YORK.

CAMBRIDGE:

H. O. HOUGHTON & CO., RIVERSIDE PRESS.

1860.

# PREFATORY REMARKS.

---

In putting before the public this Catalogue of "old masters," some explanation is due of the origin, aim, and character of the collection.

During a long residence in Europe, chiefly in Italy, the writer was led to the study of art at large, the preliminary results of which, in the shape of abstract suggestions, were given to the public in "Art-Hints," in 1855. Its favorable reception was an additional encouragement for the continuance of a pursuit, which, while so full of enjoyment to him individually, seemed also to be not without interest to his fellow-citizens generally. The historical and critical researches required for the preparation of "Art-Studies," — a work chiefly referring to the Italian schools of painting, with special reference to the æsthetic wants of America, — now in course of publication by Messrs. Derby and Jackson, New York, led to the conception of a gallery or museum of olden art for America, based upon a chronological and historical sequence of paintings, arranged according to their motives and technical progress. Without such a museum of reference, it was evident that a work on Italian art would possess but slight interest for our public; while, if formed, each would illustrate and add to the value of the other. Accordingly, he determined to attempt it. Familiar with Italian life; living in the midst of the art that was his daily study; in constant intercourse with many of the best European connoisseurs; assisted by sympathizing artistic friends, and particularly by a Greek artist, Sig. G. Mignaty, whose knowledge of the history and technical processes, combined with a keen perception and deep feeling in art, is very remarkable ; after several years of search in the highways and byways of Europe, — the writer succeeded in getting together the pictures described in this Catalogue, believing that ultimately they will be found worthy of forming the nucleus of a Free Gallery in one of our large cities, and thus be made to promote his aim, — the diffusion of artistic knowledge and æsthetic taste in America.

It is unnecessary here, though it would not be devoid of entertainment, to give a sketch of the experiences acquired in the pursuit of old pictures in Italy. In some degree, this has been done in the introductory part of " Art-Studies," under the head of "Authenticity." But in view of the very natural doubts and questionings which must arise in this country, where there exists no standard of comparison and but little critical knowledge of " old masters," there has been added to this Catalogue a series of documents, showing the estimation in which the collection is held by English, French, Italian, and American authorities. The weight of their joint opinions, to which others might be added, is, he trusts, sufficient to induce the public to give it their candid attention, without fear of being called upon to examine or enjoy works that are not *genuine*, and of the epoch and schools they profess to be. It should be kept in mind, that, for several years, they have stood the severest test possible ; to wit, the brunt of European connoisseurship in Florence, alongside of the most famous galleries known, where it has been but a step from a " masterpiece " to some characteristic specimen of the same master in this collection. At the same time, the public must not expect to find in it those masterpieces which give reputation to the great painters : they are either fixtures in the edifices for which they were painted, or have been long since absorbed into the chief public galleries, and can never be seen in America. All that he proposed to get together, was *characteristic* specimens of the schools and artists that illustrate Italian painting, in a series which should, at a glance, give a correct view of its progress from A.D. 1000 to 1600, — six centuries, embracing its rise, climax, and decadence. In no collection are all pictures of the same standard of excellence. So in this there will be found some that illustrate rather particular *motives* in art, with especial reference to its Christian inspiration, than any special technical excellence; it being part of his aim to show the topics most in vogue during past centuries. Further, the nomenclature is based upon the same system as that of the public galleries of Europe in general. But comparatively few pictures have undoubted historical pedigrees. For the rest, catalogues are the result of the best available criticism, based chiefly upon *internal* proof, sustained, where it exists, by collateral documentary evidence or trustworthy tradition. The author has conscientiously and studiously followed this system, aided by European criticism; and the Catalogue, as it now appears, is the result of several years' patient and close inquiry. Wherever he has felt there might be a diversity of opinion among critics, or he had any cause to distrust the evidence, it has been so indicated in the Catalogue; which, as a whole, will be found to be as correct as those of the galleries in Europe relied upon as authoritative. No gallery is immaculate in this respect. The severest acumen and thorough investigation cannot always decide upon technical facts hundreds of years old. All that can be required, therefore, are honesty and diligence in inquiry. Too many instances, however, occur of desire to exaggerate the importance of works of art at the expense of truth. In the Louvre and National Galleries, there are a number of pictures misnamed, without, however, materially affecting their period or school. But, in the Royal Institution at Liverpool, we find a large number of wretched specimens of old painters exalted to a rank that in Italy would excite the ridicule of the most careless observer; and in several instances, as Masaccio, Lippi, Cimabue, named without the smallest pretence to the qualities of those masters: and this spurious baptism sanctioned by the official certificates of the Committee of the Manchester Art Exhibition. Such carelessness brings disrepute upon the old masters, and misleads students.

The collection will be steadily increased and improved, as means and opportunities permit; better examples of the artists, when procured, substituted for others of a less degree of excellence ; and it depends but upon the public eventually, by their encouragement, to make of this a gallery which shall do credit to the rapidly growing artistic taste and ambition of America.    We must have our own means of æsthetic education, independent, in some degree, of Europe.    This collection is mainly important in showing that it is possible even now, when means and knowledge are practically applied, to fill, in part, the chasm that separates us so widely, in artistic enjoyment and information, from the peoples of Europe.    It is, however, but a *beginning*.

More than forty of the pictures have been engraved on copper by Vincenzo Stanghi, a pupil of Raphael Morghen, for "Art-Studies," in order to give an idea, so far as composition and general character are concerned, of the progress of art during several centuries in Italy.    Those, therefore, who cherish the " old masters," will have an opportunity, not only of studying the pictures themselves, but of taking away with them very carefully prepared outlines, with partial shadings, of many of the most interesting specimens.    It should be borne in mind, that the larger number of these paintings were *old* before America was discovered ; and necessarily they bear the marks of time.    The newness and freshness of a modern painting would be sadly out of keeping on an ancient picture.    We must accept them as they are, doing our best to get paintings as intact and well preserved as possible ; and, when repairs or restorations are necessary, limiting them to what is required to *preserve* the picture ; keeping, so far as is possible, the original tone and manner, and in no case permitting, as is too often done, entire *repainting*, which obliterates the old artist and substitutes the new.

Several of the letters given among the "Documents" are addressed to Charles Eliot Norton, Esq.    Mr. Ruskin, in a note to chap. viii., vol. v., "Modern Painters," writes of this gentleman and art-critic, "As I was correcting these pages, there was put into my hands a little work by a very dear friend, — 'Travels and Study in Italy,' by Charles Eliot Norton. I have not yet been able to do more than glance at it ; but my impression is, that by carefully reading it, together with the essay by the same writer in the ' Vita Nuova ' of Dante, a more just estimate may be formed of the religious art of Italy than by the study of any other book yet existing. At least, I have seen none in which the tone of thought was at once so tender and so just."

With such a feeling for religious art, Mr. Norton no sooner heard of the writer's collection, than he wrote to him for information as to its destination, and to others conversant with it to ascertain its character ; wishing to interest the friends of art in Boston in securing its permanent location there, with means to increase and perfect it. The replies are here appended, because Mr. Norton has not abandoned his original desire, and that they may have a wider circulation. New York, however, as the metropolitan city of America, is likely to anticipate other towns in the formation of public galleries of art. Since Mr. Norton first brought the subject, in a private way, to the notice of his friends in Boston, the collection has been largely increased in number, besides receiving some of its most precious pictures. Believing that its usefulness will be greater by appealing to the larger number of our citizens, and the prospect better of perfecting his original idea, the writer has decided to deposit it temporarily, for public exhibition, in the " Institute of Fine Arts," — a beautiful and appropriate building, lately erected by the generous enterprise of H. W. Derby, Esq., the owner of the Dusseldorf Gallery, to afford suitable facilities for bringing before the public meritorious works of art, and to promote its culture in America. It is the intention of the undersigned to devote the receipts to the increase and improvement of the gallery.

JAMES JACKSON JARVES.

September, 1860.

2

# LIST OF DOCUMENTS.

# DOCUMENTS.

## I.

*Letter of Mr. T. A. Trollope. From the London Athenæum of 12th February,* 1859.

FLORENCE, Jan. 20.

. . . . . . . . .

I was invited the other day to visit a gallery of pictures, the collection and object of which interested me much, and seemed strangely to indicate the apparently inexhaustible artistic wealth which has been stored up in these old Tuscan cities, as in a garner for the perennial supply of the entire world. They have furnished forth galleries for the delight and art-instruction of every nation of Europe ; and now they are called on to perform a similar civilizing office for the rising world on the other side of the Atlantic. And to how great an extent they are still able to answer to the demand, the collection I am speaking of most surprisingly proves. It has been brought together by an American gentleman, a Bostonian, of the name of Jarves ; and is destined to form the nucleus of a public gallery in his native city, — the young Athens of America. The funds necessary for its collection have been borrowed, I understand, by this public-spirited lover of art, of Boston, with the view of supplying his countrymen, before it is too late, with the means of obtaining a tolerably competent art-education, without the necessity of crossing the Atlantic for it. One would have thought that it had been already too late to accomplish so patriotic a purpose, were not the gallery in question here to prove the contrary. English amateurs have wistfully sounded the owner as to the possibility of tempting him to relinquish one or two of his treasures. But "the almighty dollar " has already ceased, it seems, to be almighty in Boston; for the answer was, that the collection would go unmutilated to America.

This first attempt to make the New World a sharer in the great art-heritage of Europe's old civilization is a circumstance so interesting, and, in view of the special bent the specimens obtained may give to an entire new lineage of art and artists, is so important, that it seems worth while to say a few words of the nature and merit of the collection.

Mr. Jarves has been for some years a resident in Florence, and has devoted himself entirely to this object. In the pursuit of it, Yankee energy and industry were, as a matter of course, not wanting. But the very creditable knowledge and judgment manifested in expending the funds devoted to the object, might, perhaps, have been less to be anticipated; and Boston has been very fortunate in being catered for by one of her citizens, — perhaps the only one living who has given many years of his life to the study of Italian art. But, most of all, the amazing good fortune which has helped him in his aim will strike those who can appreciate the difficulty of obtaining specimens of many of the masters, who will be well represented in the Boston gallery.

Mr. Jarves has done wisely in seeking to make his collection especially illustrative of the history, progress, and, so to speak, genealogy, of the art; being aware that it is by such a study of its masters that an artist, as distinguished from an imitator, must be formed. He has also done well in paying particular attention to the condition of his specimens; preferring to have them with the mark of time upon them, when not such as to deface the master's sense and treatment, rather than to have more showy pictures at the cost of restoration amounting to repainting.

The collection is especially rich in specimens; one or two of them almost, if not quite, unique, of the earliest days of revived art. Some very curious Byzantine works of the tenth and subsequent centuries bring the history down to Margaritone da Arezzo, in 1240, who is represented by a most remarkable altar-piece. There is also a very important picture, as an historical document, of date between 1198 and 1216, which may be found engraved in the thirteenth volume of Fumagalli's "Collection of the Principal Pictures of Europe."

Cimabue, Giotto, Duccio, Taddeo and ·Agnolo Gaddi, Andrea Orgagna, Gentile da Fabriano (a signed picture by this very rare artist, of whom not above eight works are known to be extant in Europe), Fra Angelico, Sano di Pietro, Masaccio (a fragment of a *predella* cited by Vasari), Fra Filippo Lippi, Botticelli, P. di Perugino, Lorenzo di Credi, Fra Bartolommeo (a very grand altar-piece), Leonardo da Vinci (Holy Family, with same character of background and about the same date as Lord Suffolk's *Vièrge aux Rochers*, a very valuable and undoubtedly authentic work), Lo Spagna, Sodoma (two fine specimens), Pinturicchio, Domenico and Ridolfo Ghirlandajo, Raphael (a very interesting early work, painted by him while still with his master, Perugino, from a design of his, but with variations), — all these, and several other less generally known names, are represented. There are also some interesting portraits, especially a contemporary one of Fernando Cortés; and a full-length Spanish grandee in armor, by Velasquez.

It will be admitted that no ordinary degree of good fortune must have been added to activity and judgment to render feasible the collection of such an assemblage of genuine pictures at this time of day. Those who have attempted, with more or less success, to purchase pictures recently in Italy, will probably be not a little surprised that it should have been possible; and it may be safely asserted, that if any other of the more wealthy communities of the United ·States, stimulated by the example and success of my Bostonian friend, should think, like Jack the Giant-killer's Cornish foe, "her can do that herself," and should attempt the feat with twice the pecuniary means, they will find that it is not to be repeated. And it is probable that the old Puritan city of New England will hereafter be the only community in America possessing a fair sample of ancient religious art; unless, indeed, some transatlantic Napoleon should, in the fulness of time, administer a course of *idées Napoléoniennes* to the cities of the Old World after the manner of the great original.

A very large quantity of painted canvas and wood has of late years been exported hence to the United States, to the great encouragement of our staple manufacture; but while the fact shows that the "demon," who "whispers, 'Have a taste,'" has crossed the Atlantic, the acquisitions hitherto made by the Great Republic have only proved the urgent need, that some means of instruction, such as that here provided for Boston, should be furnished to the American art-patrons who travel, as well as to the American artists who stay at home.

---

## II.

*Letter of Mr. C. C. Black, of the "Science and Art Department," South-Kensington Museum, London.*

JULY, 1859.

MY DEAR NORTON, —

When Goldsmith laid down, as one of the two rules by which a reputation for connoisseurship might be attained, that the aspirant must praise the works of Pietro Perugino, we may presume he did so not from any accurate appreciation he himself possessed of that old painter's merits, but rather that he selected the name as that of a recondite and rarely investigated luminary in the galaxy of Art. Keener eyes and better æsthetic telescopes have, however, of late years, been directed towards the pictorial sky; and Perugino's name would now stand far down, were we to catalogue the lights which shine from distances beyond the orbits even of Giotto and Cimabue, till the gazer is finally bewildered among Sienese nebulæ and Byzantine star-dust. These thoughts came on me forcibly, on crossing the Piazza Maria Antonia, after a by no means thorough examination of the very interesting collection formed by our friend J. J. Jarves. Although I think you visited it, when in Florence some years ago, his untiring energy has added to it so largely since you were among us, that I am minded to give you (without much pretence to chronological accuracy) some notes of a few chief objects of my admiration.

Though aware that Mr. Jarves had confined his purchases principally to the more ancient masters, proposing — and wisely — to illustrate the germ and growth of Modern Art, I was not prepared for the distance to which skill and patience have carried him back; and found him, to my surprise, the possessor of one of the earliest known representations of the Crucifixion, dating from the tenth, or possibly the ninth, century. By the way, in writing to one who is acquainted with the galleries of the Catacombs, I may enter a *caveat* against the accusation of inaccuracy, by explaining that I mean one of the earliest *movable* representations; excluding, of course, wall-paintings. Specimens of this date are naturally very rare : some, however, there are, and well authenticated; one, in particular, in the Museum of Fine Arts at Florence, closely resembling this of Mr. Jarves. A marked and distinctive peculiarity is the form of the cross; which, indeed, can be termed so merely for convenience, as it is Y-shaped, curiously resembling the embroidery on a priestly stole, and figuring, moreover, in the shield of the Archbishop of Canterbury. To step from this strange relic of early piety to Margaritone of Arezzo may not be strictly chronological; but, as I said before, this I do not profess to be. This old master is represented here by a Virgin, attended by the saints Peter and Paul; the central painting surrounded with smaller ones, which show various events of their lives. Their martyrdoms in particular are packed with an economy of space truly wonderful. In singular contrast to the hard, rugged, Ben-Jonsonish energy of Margaritone, is a Greek painting of very early date (well known to collectors, and engraved by Fumagalli), highly finished in detail; the jewels of the tiara and the folds of embroidered drapery quite wonderful; but the features smooth, polished, and insignificant as one of Hayley's poems. I was much pleased with a small Giovanni di Paolo, representing a female saint in gray, who kneels to a pope. How these old artists caught the key-note of character in their figures! It seems as though there was in the childhood of Art something analogous to the actual childhood of human life; for even as an observant child unfailingly selects the chief characteristic, bodily or mental, of a visitor, so do we find these early painters insisting on distinctive character as determinately as though they had just been reading the "Ars Poetica." We have here a demure train-bearer and a sulky cardinal, both of whom I have seen in Roman processions, — Corpus Domini, for instance, — times without number.

Duccio, whose noble picture at Siena hangs on the Cathedral wall so awkwardly as to be hardly visible, may be admired here much more satisfactorily in a beautiful Virgin and Child, as also in a Crucifixion; showing what, to me, was a somewhat novel treatment of this much-worn subject. The chief personage among the spectators is a Roman soldier, in all the gorgeous panoply of war, *sagum, paludamentum*, etc., etc.; whose attitude of determination somewhat puzzled me till I bethought me of the centurion (called, by the church of Rome, "Longinus") who declared, "Truly, this man was the Son of God!" If any doubt could exist, it would be removed by noticing the countenance of the soldier behind him. Wonder, horror, and the reserve generated by discipline, are all combined in his attitude; and we may clearly see his consciousness, that what in his captain may be but an unguarded word, would in him be flat blasphemy. Perhaps no better example could be found, to show the soul these early masters put into their works, than the various expressions, gestures, and costumes here displayed on a space not larger than a sheet of letter-paper.

A Virgin and Child with a Goldfinch, which hangs near the Duccio, shows how much the Italian painters followed each other; or were possibly all led, by some now obsolete tradition, in the accompaniments to their chief figures. This work is ascribed, doubtfully, to Giotto; who, however, contributes one indubitable Entombment. There is a Cimabue, genuine in style, and genuine in subject too, as representing one of those delightful facts which occurred only in the "good old times," — St. Nicholas throwing gold balls into the windows of poor, portionless maidens. You have Santa Claus still among you, and can tell whether he yet indulges in that beneficent play. I fear that the acquaintance our English poor have with gilded balls is of a less pleasing character.

Fra Angelico appears here unmistakably in a painting of

three saints,—St. Zenobio, St. Francis, and St. Thomas (I forget which of them); and an Adoration of the Magi, by Simone Memmi, would attract any one's notice, if only from a wonderful group of men, horses, and camels, thrust together in much-admired disorder. Some such group may have been seen by Shakspeare, in his mind's eye or otherwise, when he wrote the description of the tapestry in the "Rape of Lucrece," where "for Achilles' image stood a spear grasped in an armed hand."

I have really no time to expatiate on the various excellent specimens of painters, good and rare; such as, Pietro Cavallini, Andrea Castagno, Matteo da Siena, — of whom we have a Virgin and Child, and happily not his oft-repeated and horribly elaborated Murder of the Innocents, — Taddeo Gaddi, who shows us St. Dominic receiving at the hands of Peter the sword he used so ruthlessly against heretics. Nor can I do more than offer to more leisurely speculation two quaint Byzantine tablets, in which Julian the Apostate is being speared by Mercourios (?); while Maxentius undergoes the same fate at the hand, not of Constantine, but of one Dicaterina, — St. Catharine, I suppose; but let it pass. I must, however, do homage to Sano di Pietro; an artist whose works, even in Italy, must be sought with care, as nearly all the best are confined to his native city of Siena. Nevertheless, we find here no less than three specimens of his handiwork, — an Adoration of Magi; a St. Margaret, wonderful in drapery; and a Coronation of the Virgin, so pure and sacred in feeling as to show at once his right to the title of the Sienese Fra Angelico. Of Benozzo Gozzoli there is an Annunciation, in a state of preservation very uncommon; and the same subject by Credi, clean and fresh in coloring as all his works are, and treated in a very pleasing, unconventional manner.

"*Omnia ex ovo*," says the old physiological adage: and I presume that the Virgin Mary herself forms no exception to the rule; unless, indeed, the dogma of the Immaculate Conception interfere, — a question which I beg to refer to his Holiness Pio Nono. At all events, here we have the Virgin, very pleasingly painted by a scholar of Albertinelli, enclosed in an egg, — not a *vesica piscis* glory, nor an oval mass of clouds; but a veri-

3

tably well-painted egg, — the shell broken open at the side ; the
fractured edges carefully drawn, so as to display the figure.
Leaving unsolved the mystic meaning of this very pretty picture, I pass to another Virgin and Child, delicate in coloring
and charming in expression, by Sandro Botticelli ; and to a small
panel, liable to be overlooked by a casual observer, but very
interesting, as being not improbably the identical Birth of St.
John, painted by Masaccio, and described in Vasari. The cir-
cumstantial evidence, with which I shall not trouble you, is very
strong in its favor.

You know the man of many names, — Sodoma to the world,
Razzi of Siena to his familiars ; and now, by favor of some of
those confounded investigators who upset our faith in Romulus,
Richard, Joan of Arc, — nay, even would do so in respect to
Shakspeare himself, — Bazzi of Piedmont would seem to be
the genuine name of the painter. Happily, these *rixæ de lana
caprinâ* are very unimportant. The names may perish ; but
Romeo, Lear, Hamlet, and, though in a humbler sphere, the
Chapel of San Bernardino at Siena and the upper floor of the
Farnesina at Rome, are undeniable facts. Mr. Jarves possesses
a glorious Razzi, — Christ bearing the Cross, — almost as rich
in coloring as the grand fresco in the Belle Arti at Siena, and
decidedly nobler in expression, — the point in which Sodoma
was most commonly weak. A proof of this assertion may be
seen by comparing his celebrated St. Catharine Fainting, in the
Dominican Church at Siena, with the same subject as treated
by Beccafumi in this gallery. Although in many points closely
resembling, and generally to the advantage of Sodoma, the countenance of the Father, in Beccafumi's work, is far grander.

Do you remember the shops of the *pizzicaroli* at Rome
during Passion Week, — those mysterious caverns propped by
sides of bacon, panelled with hams, and roofed with numerous
starry lamps twinkling from a heaven of lard ? If not, read
Hans Andersen's " Improvisatore ; " or look with me at a picture of Masolino da Panicale, where the Virgin is adoring her
new-born infant in front of just such a cave. Though meant
for stone, the brown walls and whitish roof bear unmistakable
traces of their adipose porcine models. Germany, ever anxious

to get a foothold in Italy, here sends, as her representative, a Crucifixion, richly colored, carefully executed, and showing a wonderfully elaborate background, where Jerusalem appears crowded with steep roofs, golden weathercocks, and pepper-box turrets. Truly, the early Germans were no more solicitous as to anachronisms than the later Italians; as witness a Crucifixion here by Paolo Veronese. The painter has somewhat softened the painful character of this subject by the compassionate air which he has given to the warrior.

But I find my letter has already run to an unconscionable length. I have left myself no room to speak at all, as it deserves, of what is, perhaps, the most valuable gem of the whole gallery, — an undoubted Leonardo da Vinci. You, who know that Leonardos are so rare that they may in general terms be declared quite unattainable, — albeit they figure in every catalogue as surely as Johannisberger in a Rhine-steamer's wine-list, — will be glad to learn that Migliarini, whose judgment cannot be called in question, adds the weight of his authority to the preponderating historical evidence of the authenticity of this work.

I should like to detail to you some of the gorgeous court-costumes devised by Paolo Uccello to grace the pageant where King Solomon, in all his glory, meets the Queen of Sheba; to speculate on the interpretation of a most perplexing and enticing allegory by Gentile da Fabriano, called the "Triumph of Love;" and to speak more fully than is now possible of a beautiful female head by Cesare da Sesto, of a soldierly Velasquez, of a large and important Ridolfo Ghirlandajo.

Before concluding this very imperfect review, in which I have left quite unmentioned many interesting pictures, let me revert to our old friend Perugino, with whose name I began my letter, and of whom Mr. Jarves possesses a small but unmistakably genuine painting; as also to our dearer friend Noll Goldsmith, whose other recipe was, "to observe that the picture would have been better if the painter had taken more pains." How very safely this remark may yet be applied to the Caracci and their school! Rarely, if ever, do we meet a work of the Bolognese school, which does not, in spite of its unquestionable merit, offend by a certain careless air, which seems to show that the painter felt himself fully equal, nay, possibly superior, to the requirements of his subject.  On the other hand, the conscientious labor, the solemn purity, visible in every portion of a painting by Duccio, Fra Angelico, or Sano di Pietro, impress on us the conviction, that these men felt called on to make a holocaust of the talent God had given them, in serving, as best they could, the Giver.

I must now conclude ; and only hope that this imperfect summary may suffice to show what can be done, even at this late period of picture-hunting, when good judgment and activity are backed by patience and well-timed liberality.

C. C. Black.

---

III.

*Extract from the "Revista di Firenze," August, 1859, — the Art-Journal of Tuscany, — written by Sig. Guidici, Professor of Æsthetics in the Academy of Florence.  Translated from the Italian.*

It is related, that, a few years since, a certain person, having collected a considerable number of works of art with the object of making a lucrative speculation, determined to take them to America.  He said to himself, " My merchandise will obtain a much higher price in that young, rich, and prosperous country, than I can hope to get for it in any European city."  But the poor man reckoned without his host.

Having arrived in one of the most populous, opulent, and cultivated maritime cities of the United States, he exposed his pictures — which, I know not whether correctly or otherwise, bore the most celebrated names in the history of the arts — to public inspection.  But the public understood nothing of such matters; and the unfortunate merchant was obliged to carry back his precious freight to old Europe.  He stated, that, having visited the houses of several reputed lovers of art, he saw nothing else hanging on the walls of their saloons than a few portraits, God knows how painted; and pictures representing ships of every form and size. He therefore concluded that art in the New World, generally speaking, was a book which no one either studies or cares to study.

Supposing that our merchant's deluded hopes induced him to exaggerate, it is, however, undeniable, that the taste for the fine arts is a rare exception among Americans; and it is equally certain, that in no one of the principal centres of civilization does there exist any collection of works in which rising genius is enabled to study, without feeling the necessity of crossing the Atlantic to visit us, in order to render itself worthy of forming the future artist. This is certainly a great pity ; since, in every country, art would find a soil, in which, if properly planted, it might revive, take root, and flourish with fresh vigor.

We are now happy to announce that this deficiency is about to be remedied ; or, at least, a first step to be taken to secure the accomplishment of this desirable object. Mr. Jarves, a native of Boston, who has for several years resided in Florence, has, with the intelligence of a real connoisseur and the affection of a warm patriot, commenced forming a collection which he intends to offer to that city, in order that it may become the nucleus of a gallery, which, when the culture of the arts has once been developed in those parts, might increase, and in time, possibly, arrive at perfection. With the intention of exhibiting to his countrymen the rise, progress, and perfection of painting in Italy, Mr. Jarves has collected a considerable number of the works of the old masters, from the times designated " Byzantine," up to the sixteenth century. In this gallery are paintings, more or less preserved, of Margaritone d'Arezzo, Cimabue, Giotto, Duccio, Taddeo and Agnolo Gaddi, Orgagna, Gentile da Fabbriano, Fra Angelico, Masaccio ; Sano di Pietro, a celebrated painter of Siena ; Fra Filippo Lippi, Sandro Botticelli, Lorenzo di Credi, Fra Bartolommeo della Porta, Spagna, Sodoma, Pinturicchio, Domenico and Ridolfo del Ghirlandajo, Pietro Perugino, Leonardo da Vinci, Raphael, and others, — celebrated names, supported by which, a new enterprise cannot fail to succeed.

It has been a hundred times repeated, that, for more than half a century, works of art of every kind have been exported from Tuscany to enrich the public and private galleries of Europe. Notwithstanding these incalculable exportations, numerous are the still remaining treasures, that Mr. Jarves has been enabled to unite thus many admirable works. The thought that Italy will have to lose these, awakens a melancholy feeling; but it is, nevertheless, consolatory to know that their contributing to the culture of a great people will be a fresh argument to prove that Italy, even in her present unhappy political condition, has never ceased to awaken and diffuse civilization in every part of the known world.

---

## IV.

*Letter of Sig. Bucci, Inspector of the Uffizi Gallery, Florence. Translated from the Italian.*

MR. JARVES.

DEAR SIR, — I have long been acquainted with your praiseworthy design of making, without regard to cost or trouble, a collection of paintings of our older Tuscan schools, in order to show how these masters prepared the way for the very excellent artists who lived in the sixteenth century, and to transport the same to America, to make known by examples in that remote region, just risen so high in the scale of civilization, the character of the primitive masters of art, and how they were able to make painting attain so eminent a position.

However little the paintings of these masters may be appreciated by a people accustomed, for the most part, to the sight of works of mere illusion and pleasure to the eye, yet the paintings carried by you to America cannot fail of being of great benefit to artists, and institutions of education.

I congratulate you, Mr. Jarves, upon a selection, which, from its excellence, must have cost you much persevering research and money. Your politeness has enabled me, before your departure, to examine all your paintings; and among the number, by no means small, of excellent ones, permit me to especially notice, as very remarkable and rare, even among us, and of our own school, "The Rape of Dejanira," by Antonio

Pollajuolo ; that beautiful " Madonna and Child," by Sandro Botticelli ; St. Girolomo, by Fra Filippo Lippi ; the " Annunciation," by Lorenzo di Credi ; the " Sacra Familia," by Lo Spagna, a scholar of Perugino ; the " Holy Family," by Domenico Ghirlandajo ; and a small and extremely rare and valuable picture of the " Adoration of the Magi," by Luca Signorelli.

Among later paintings of other schools, I admired a magnificent portrait by Diego Velasquez ; and the " Crucifixion," by Rubens.

Permit me, then, before you leave our city, in attestation of my esteem, to contribute my feeble praise and congratulation for the efforts you have made for the advantage of art in your native country.

With, &c., &c., &c.,

EMILIO BUCCI,<br>Inspector of the Uffizi Gallery of Florence.

———

V.

*Extract of a Letter from Mons. A. F. Rio, of Paris, the well-known author of " Poetry of Christian Art," and " Life of Leonardo da Vinci."*

MY DEAR SIR, — I have not the least hesitation in declaring that I fully believe it [the Leonardo] to be the work of that great master. I cannot help envying your good luck in making such a valuable acquisition. You could not begin your collection under better auspices. The genuine pictures of Leonardo are so rare, that the want of one has left, to this day, a sore gap in the gallery of many a sovereign.

You are quite right in trying to get pictures of the Sienese school, which has been, till now, less studied than the others, and which is growing more and more into repute. Your two pictures of Antonio Razzi (Sodoma) are quite sufficient to give an idea of that great painter, who has so often been compared with Raphael himself ; but my weakness for the old school impels me to say, that, for my own gratification, I should prefer your pictures of Sano di Pietro. A time will come when that charming master will be appreciated to his full value, and his works sought after as so many precious gems of mystical thought. France, England, and Germany know him only by reputation. I do not remember seeing a single picture of his in any of those countries. The specimen which you possess has two great advantages : it represents the painter's favorite subject, — the Coronation of the Virgin, — and is in a perfect state of preservation. I have observed in your collection a charming little picture by Matteo di Giovanni. Your Gentile da Fabriano is, on account of its date, an important document in the history of that school; and I should place still higher the Madonna between four Saints, by Lo Spagna, who was the best pupil of Perugino, next to Raphael.

You will render the science of art more accessible to those [in America] who cannot cross the seas to study it in its birth-place.

With the best wishes for the success of your patriotic under-taking,

Most sincerely yours,

RIO.

---

VI.

*Extract from a Letter of the Baron Hector Garriod, a well-known European connoisseur, formerly commissioned by the Kings of Holland and Sardinia to purchase paintings for their galleries, and a writer on art. Translated from the French.*

I congratulate you, Mr. Jarves, upon having that charming "Virgin." For a long time, some people will dispute whether it belongs to Leonardo or to his school only ; which last, no one can doubt.

Now, the school of Leonardo is something more than the mechanical continuation of painters producing original works : it is rather the personification of a creative mind, that had little time to spare for the execution of its theories, and which most frequently put them into form only by the co-operation of those whom it instructed. Even when Leonardo undertook a work, the hour of its completion seldom arrived. His school may be considered as himself under different points of view, and at different stages of completion; for, where his hand did not labor, his mind governed.

Of easel-pictures, some ultra severe judges allow, as solely his, only two, — the " Medusa " and " Joconda ; " thus putting themselves, on one side, out of the reach of a mistake. For my own part, I am the more liberal towards my own enjoyment, without believing that I wound the glory of a master whose too limited fame I should take pleasure in extending ; but holding even to the severity of the most exclusive judges, and taking, as a standard of comparison, the indisputable " Medusa," I find evidence for asserting that your " Virgin " belongs to the pencil of Leonardo himself. The peculiarities of manipulation, firmness of touch, strength of modelling ; the sharpness of outline, left incomplete in the eyes, mouth, and other parts of the face, either because the painter put off its completion indefinitely, or that he dreaded lest the firmness of his design should be too prominent in the magic vagueness he sought in his chiaroscuro, — are all of him rather than of his scholars.

The tone also of your painting — " *un brun ardoisé* " — is that peculiar hue of Leonardo's, — his " *œuil de couleur*," — which connects itself particularly with the chemical and scientific processes of that great man. The tone of his imitators is quite different. With Luini it is golden, violet with Solario, brilliant and Raphael-like with Cesare da Sesto, reddish with Marco D'Oggione and Beltraffio, and too free and *caracterisé* with Giovanoni or Sodoma to be confounded with his.

I dare to predict for you a signal success in the arena which your painting deserves to enter, and to dispute with a very small number of concurrents the coveted honors of so elevated a rank. I take pleasure in telling you this at the moment when I see, for the last time, the beautiful specimen you carry off beyond the seas, like an unacclimated flower. My memory will follow you both with sentiments of sincere interest. ، . . .

&c., &c., &c.,

H. Gabriod.

## VII.

*Article from the "Boston Courier," Feb. 9, 1859, containing letters from Sir Charles Eastlake, Director of the National Gallery, London; and the Chevalier M. A. Migliarini, Director of the Florentine Gallery.*

It will be remembered, that, a few weeks ago, there appeared in our columns a letter from a correspondent in Florence, speaking in very high terms of a collection of pictures, especially of the works of the early Italian artists, made by our townsman, Mr. James Jackson Jarves. Mr. Jarves has been for some years engaged in gathering together his acquisition; and his intention is to continue in the same pursuit for some years longer, not with a view of accumulating a valuable collection which shall be held for the exclusive gratification of himself and his friends and transmitted to his heirs, but with higher aims and ends. He wishes to employ it in such a way as to promote a taste for art, and the cultivation of art, among his countrymen; and, having been born and reared in Boston, he naturally prefers that his collection should have a resting-place here. His desire is, that it form the nucleus of a Free Gallery of Art, for the benefit of the public and the instruction of artists. The possession of such a gallery in combination with our Public Library, and the splendid Museum of Natural History which is destined to be reared at once in our immediate neighborhood, would give to Boston peculiar advantages for bestowing upon its citizens that finished education which includes science, literature, and the fine arts, and make it proportionally attractive to strangers. In a community like ours, where wealth and political distinction are so eagerly pursued, — neither object of pursuit being very elevating or refining in its effects, — a public gallery of works of art would shed a benignant and beneficent influence over all that came within its sphere, and thus tend to correct the hardening and narrowing tendencies which so much beset us.

With this view, we have much pleasure in bringing this collection again to the notice of our readers, and in laying before them some testimony which proves, beyond question or cavil, its merit and importance. The first piece that we offer is a letter addressed to Mr. Jarves by Sir Charles Eastlake, President of the Royal Academy, — a gentleman cautious alike by temperament and official position, and whose words may be fairly taken, therefore, to mean a little more than they say.

7, FITZROY SQUARE, LONDON, Nov. 16, 1858.

DEAR SIR, — I rejoice to hear that you propose to send your collection of specimens of early Italian masters, in its entire state, to America. Few would have taken the trouble you have gone through in discovering and obtaining these works. Your continued residence in Tuscany has enabled you to avail yourself of many excellent opportunities. Good fortune has also sometimes rewarded you; but to your discrimination and knowledge your success is chiefly to be ascribed.

I consider that the series in question would form an excellent foundation for a gallery of Italian art; and I trust, that, in your native country, it will be appreciated, and kept together. I purposely avoid particularizing any works, because I have at all times uniformly declined to give any kind of certificate as regards single pictures; but I can conscientiously congratulate you on the formation of the collection as a whole. I believe that many valuable additions have been made to it even since I saw it.

Wishing you all success in your patriotic object, I am, dear sir,

Your faithful servant,

C. L. EASTLAKE.

JAMES J. JARVES, Esq.

We next present a translation of a communication addressed to Mr. Jarves by Prof. Migliarini, Director of the Uffizi Gallery, — an artist of merit, and probably the very highest authority on art in Italy. His observations are mostly confined to a single picture in Mr. Jarves's collection, which he affirms to be an original Leonardo da Vinci; and, if so, we need not say that it is a possession of great rarity and great value. The technical and scientific character of Prof. Migliarini's remarks, though it may make them less interesting to the general reader, will, we trust, commend them all the more to our artist-friends.

FLORENCE, GALLERY OF THE UFFIZI, Oct. 15, 1858.

MY DEAR MR. JARVES, — I hope you will allow me to express my satisfaction at the pleasure afforded me of admiring, on two different occasions, your rich collection of ancient paintings, in the acquisition of which it appears to me that a great deal has been owing to good fortune; for, without this, perseverance and money would have been of little avail.

I will not enumerate the many different artists of whom you have obtained beautiful specimens, such as Cimabue, the Giotteschi, followed by Dello, il Pollajuolo, il Ghirlandajo, and many others; but, among so many, I will confine myself to that gem of Leonardo da Vinci, which it seems to me incredible that you should have been able to fall in with and possess.

Every one knows that Da Vinci lived long, but, unfortunately, did little in painting; his attention having been distracted by the fortuitous circumstances in life, and more by the many other sciences he professed, in which he was also distinguished as a great genius. There are thus many galleries which boast of possessing some of his productions: but to the experienced eye of the connoisseur it very often happens, that, in view of the object decorated with so great a name, preconceived expectation of enjoyment is followed by the silent apathy of indifference; and this all the more because he had disciples of great merit, who imitated him with much ability.

One of the striking peculiarities of your picture is, that it is unfinished: and in this condition it best proves its true originality; for, if one of Leonardo's best imitators had copied it, — while there could be no doubt in regard to the design, well known to be that of Leonardo, and his drawing of the Infant Saviour, "il Bambino," is well known, — he would have carried it to completion, either for pecuniary benefit, or gain in reputation.

But here I may be asked, if a copyist in such a case could not have left his copy unfinished. I am willing to admit this; but would ask my inquirer to reflect, that whoever undertakes Leonardo's very difficult method of laying on the body-colors would not dare to imitate those occasional dashes of the pencil, of which there appear clear indications in your picture, seeming to be mere memoranda for changes to be afterwards made at pleasure. He who copies so great an artist has always before his eyes the almost impossibility of imitating him, and consequently lacks the courage to paint with entire freedom.

Moreover, let it pass as a general rule, that all the imitators of Leonardo are apt to be low-toned; yet the lowest tone is never black: in its gradation towards the light, it always inclines to the hue of bistre or tobacco color. This peculiar characteristic, it seems to me, had its origin in the experience which the most able masters of that time had in the bad effects of lamp-black, employed by Leonardo, and afterwards by Giulio Romano. These substituted other blacks, which, mixed with other colors, produce a shade tint.* On examination, your picture has no such appearance, but is really coal-black in the deep shadows, as is always the case with the works known to be of Da Vinci.

I shall probably be reminded of another style of Leonardo's; namely, that of his portraits, in which this intense blackness is seldom found. And this is quite natural, because he treated historical subjects in a different manner from portrait-painting. In his "Treatise on Painting," he often advises the sitter to be placed in a broad light, so that the features may not be cut up by too violent shadows. Is it possible that he would recommend to others what he did not practise himself? Hence it follows, that, in a broad light, he could dispense with the pernicious use of black; and, for this reason, many of his portraits are lighter, and better preserved.

It is needless for me to enlarge on the beauties of this painting, as this would lead me into long digressions; and I should not wish to describe qualities of which it is impossible to give an approximate idea with the pen. I will only remark, that the landscape is composed of many minute features, finished with great minuteness, in order that the figures of the Virgin and the Child may, by contrast, gain in grandeur of effect.

---

* The mixture of black, in the shadows, was soon found by experience to be a very pernicious practice, because the black gradually comes to the surface, obscuring the other colors with which it was mixed; and subsequent artists made it a rule to exclude black entirely from their shadows. Instead of black, they used a mixture of deep transparent colors, — blue, red, and yellow, mixed to a neutral tint.

I will not mention Leonardo's peculiar grace, and sweetness of expression, which have been frequently dilated upon by eminent writers. I will say nothing of the wonderful relief of his *chiaroscuro*, of which language cannot give the slightest idea.

I therefore conclude, congratulating you on so beautiful and precious an acquisition; and, begging you to receive kindly this expression of my admiration, I am, with many thanks for your civility,

Yours, etc.,

M. A. MIGLIARINI.

---

VIII.

*Extract from Mrs. H. Beecher Stowe's Letter to C. E. Norton, Esq.*

ANDOVER, July 30, 1860.

I was greatly interested in Mr. Jarves's gallery last winter, which I visited many times, and studied with great care. I was specially interested in mediæval and pre-Raphaelite art, which had more real power over me than any thing I ever saw before, imperfect as it was in technical execution. Mr. Jarves's collection is certainly a fine one, even for Italy, — fine in the neighborhood of the Belle Arti. What, then, would it be for Boston!

The one Leonardo, undoubted though unfinished, is to me one of the most *interesting* pictures I ever saw, as illustrating that artist's peculiar power of producing the mysterious expression of depth and divinity in a downcast eye; and is so interestingly, in its treatment, like the head of the Saviour in the Last Supper, at Milan, that I could not but think it one of the studies he made when he was working up his idea of that grand subject. The pictures by Sodoma, I thought most valuable specimens; but it would take too long to particularize.

I think, as a historical series, and a nucleus around which a collection may gather, it is incredibly good : only very *peculiar* advantages could have put it in his hands. This opinion is shared by Prof. Rio, by Mr. and Mrs. Trollope ; indeed, by the most competent persons with whom I conversed. I ardently hope Boston may secure it : it will be an eternal shame to our country if such an opportunity is lost.

---

## IX.

*Letter from Mr. Trollope, addressed to Mrs. H. Beecher Stowe.*

FLORENCE, Jan. 16, 1860.

MY DEAR MADAM, — In reply to your inquiries respecting Mr. Jarves's gallery of ancient pictures, I am happy to be able, with great confidence, to assure you that they are genuine pictures, the productions of the great masters to whom they are assigned, as far as can be known by the critical skill of several of the best judges in Europe. Some have, of course, been restored ; but by no means more than is usually the case with works of such antiquity.

I beg to be understood as saying this, *not* as the result of any critical examination of the pictures by myself, for I have no such artistic knowledge as would make my opinion of any value ; but I have known, for many years, the artist by whose assistance Mr. Jarves brought together a portion of his very remarkable collection, and I know him to be a most strictly honorable and upright man. This, in addition to my knowledge of Mr. Jarves himself, is the best possible guaranty for the authenticity of the works in question. It is, however, within my knowledge, that other very competent judges have considered the collection an extremely remarkable and valuable one.

I send you the article of mine in the " Athenæum," which you wished to see, and which I most assuredly should not have written, had I not had the means of feeling sure that the collection was a genuine one.

I am, my dear madam, very cordially yours,

T. ADOLPHUS TROLLOPE.

## X.

*Letter of Hon. William B. Kinney, formerly American Minister at Turin, and for seven years a resident at Florence, engaged in artistic and historical studies.*

FLORENCE, June 3, 1860.

It would be superfluous, if not presuming, to offer you, dear Mr. Jarves, the impressions of a mere amateur, touching your admirable collection of ancient paintings. But assuredly it cannot be presumptuous to say, as I am most happy in being able to do from personal knowledge, that it has been cordially approved, at various times, by artists and connoisseurs of the very highest repute, — critics whose concurring opinions would be received in all European circles as final and conclusive.

You may, therefore, safely be congratulated on the remarkable success of your long researches; for no one could have anticipated that so rare a collection, especially rich in early Christian art, could have been gleaned, at this late day, in the often explored by-ways of Italy.

Surely the friends of art at home will promply respond to your liberal proposals; and the country may then rejoice in an acquisition which would be considered a public treasure in any capital of Europe. Such an opportunity of founding an historic gallery of art — an important institution in a country constantly exposed to the rudest influences — may never occur again. All our friends here, who appreciate the value of art, heartily commend your enterprise.

Very truly, &c.,

WM. B. KINNEY.

Mr. J. J. JARVES.

---

## XI.

*Letters of Hon. Charles Sumner. "Boston Transcript," Aug. 2, 1850; and Sept. 12, 1860.*

A prominent place among those who have taken deep interest in the movement should be awarded to Mr. J. J. Jarves, whose pen and personal influence have been largely devoted to the subject, in a way to secure the co-operation of gentlemen interested in the fine arts. The following extract, from a recent letter from the Hon. Charles Sumner, furnishes the latest intelligence in regard to this important matter. The words of Mr. Sumner will be read with much satisfaction by the people of Boston. He says, —

"I write from the great interest I feel in the plans of Mr. Jarves, who is now making, in Florence, a collection of pictures, which he hopes may be the beginning of a Public Gallery in Boston. The idea is noble ; and I do not doubt that such a gallery, if successfully organized, would add effectively to the means of education in our community. Is not this true ? Surely the complement of the Public Library is a Public Gallery.

"The collection, thus far, is confined chiefly to the early schools of Florence and Siena ; but, as far as it goes, it is singularly successful. This I say, after having examined it with care. In short, it is an admirable beginning : some of the pictures are of great beauty, and all are important in the history of Art.

"I offer my testimony, founded on actual observation, to the value and felicity of this collection."

BOSTON, 12th September, 1860.

MY DEAR SIR, — I have too long delayed my acknowledgment of the pleasure which I had in seeing again the pictures you kindly showed me at your house in Boston. But, much as I enjoyed those specimens, the pleasure was enhanced by the souvenirs of the whole collection to which they belong. This it was my good fortune to see at Florence.

I cannot conceal my astonishment that you have been able to bring together a collection of such surpassing historic and artistic interest. To a student, in our country, of the great Italian school of painting, it must be invaluable ; and, as the beginning of a gallery of art, I hope, from the bottom of my heart, that it may be secured for Boston. It contains pictures of which, I think, any gallery might be proud ; and also specimens of certain masters, which, if now allowed to slip away, may not come again within our reach.

It would be useless for me to specify pictures which arrested my attention; but I take the liberty of adding, that, while enjoying very much several exquisite works, I was especially impressed by the collection as a whole, illustrative of a most important period in art.

I doubt not you have already had pleasure, as you surely must have had work, in making this collection; but I trust that yet another pleasure will be yours, in the gratitude of an enlightened community, freely rendered towards one who has so quietly, faithfully, and bountifully contributed to improve its taste and enlarge its knowledge. At all events, you have my best wishes for your success, with assurances of the regard with which I am, my dear sir,

Sincerely yours,

CHARLES SUMNER.

J. J. JARVES, Esq.

---

## XII.

*Extract from a Letter of Miss Hosmer to C. E. Norton, Esq.*

AUG. 5, 1860.

I may venture to express an opinion of Mr. Jarves's collection of pictures, as I have had several opportunities of examining it in Florence; and I am happy in having this occasion of testifying to their great beauty and value.

Apart from the merit of individual pictures, this collection, it seems to me, would be of the highest value in this country, as it shows the progress of art in different schools, from the earliest date down to the period when it attained its greatest perfection; each school being represented by very perfect and beautiful specimens.

As far as I am aware, no such historic gallery of paintings as this exists in our country, — certainly none so rich; and, when we consider the great difficulty of obtaining such a collection, — a difficulty which increases year by year, — I feel sure that it would be a source of sincere regret to all her true lovers of art, if Boston failed to secure a prize which would place her Athenæum at the head of all art-galleries in America.

It gives me great pleasure also to make known to you the opinion of Sir Charles Eastlake, who spoke to me of these paintings in terms of admiration, and who was much impressed with their value to students and to those who would make themselves familiar with the various styles of the old masters.

Truly yours,

H. F. HOSMER.

---

## XIII.

### *Letter from Louis Thies, Esq.*

Mr. Thies is well known among connoisseurs in Europe and America for his successful exertions in getting together and arranging the Gray collection of engravings, lately bequeathed to Harvard University. Having been formed, without regard to expense, by the late public-spirited owner, it is the finest and most complete in our country, and is excelled by few only in Europe. Not only do we find in it the best impressions of the most celebrated engravers, but some of extreme rarity: one by Finiguerra, the father of Italian engraving, if not the European inventor, which is considered as *unique*, and would command a price that would startle the uninitiated in these matters. This collection is accessible to the student of art through the courtesy of the curator; and it does for the history of engraving that which I have sought to do for painting.

Mr. Thies, having devoted a lifetime to the study of art, with the advantages of a European education, is well qualified to speak on the subject. To an enthusiastic feeling for his pursuit, he joins the critical acumen and patient inquiry which distinguish his former compatriots and students of art, Rumohr, Kugler, Passavant, and Förster.

It may be of interest to the American amateur to know that there is attached to the Gray collection a valuable library of works on art, for reference. J. J. J.

CAMBRIDGE COLLEGE, Sept. 13, 1860.

MY DEAR SIR, — I cannot help expressing to you the very great pleasure I had in being permitted to see, on several occasions lately, the specimens of the old Italian masters which you had the kindness to show me. I certainly never looked forward to seeing in America pictures of such great merit and value.

The Perugino — Baptism of Christ — is extremely characteristic of that master, and is one of his most pleasing compositions. The upper part — the Almighty with the angels — recalls to me Raphael's fresco in San Severo, Perugia, in which he borrowed this upper part from his master ; only that, in your picture, the principal figure holds a globe instead of a book.

The Lorenzo di Credi Crucifixion pleases me still more. I think it is one of the most charming little pictures the master ever produced. The figure of the Saviour is wonderfully fine, and the expression of the Magdalen at his feet embodies the poetry of grief.

The portrait of the Princess Vitelli, by Franc. Francia, is a remarkable picture, most charming in the landscape. It is beautiful in modelling, warm in color, and with those peculiar characteristics that please so much in Raphael's earlier pictures. The picture would be an acquisition to any public gallery, on account of the great rarity of the master, as well as for the subject.

Luca Signorelli is a still rarer master. Your specimen, the Adoration of the Magi, is as perfect a one as I have ever seen, and admirably represents the peculiarities of the artist. It is particularly valuable for its fine condition.

It would take too long to particularize all the pictures worthy of mention, even among those of your collection which you were able to let me see.

But your Leonardo da Vinci much surpassed my expectations. It is a picture of the highest order. One recognizes the hand of the master in the modelling, which might be called plastic ; his wonderful force and beauty of chiaroscuro ; harmonious treatment of colors ; strength of touch, and other points, which characterize him as the greatest of masters. Your picture, in these respects, does not represent merely a type of his works, but absolutely his manner and design. The background reminds me of the Viérge aux Rochers, which is considered the most pleasing of his Holy Families. If Boston can secure this one picture, we need not envy either the Louvre or Lord Suffolk theirs.

No doubt the Leonardo is the most valuable painting in your collection; but the one that will be the most popular is that beautiful Murillo, the subject of which seems to me to be Erigone. The delicate, silvery tone of the flesh, and the wonderfully harmonized colors of the whole, produce an effect like a beautiful strain of music, and call to my mind some of the charming Correggios in Dresden.

I should regret deeply to have such a collection as this not secured for Boston, — a collection which does so much credit to the taste and erudition of the collector, and which would be the pride of his native town.

Hoping I may soon have an opportunity to see the entire collection, I remain truly yours,

Louis Thies.

## XIV.

*Correspondence of the "Boston Courier" of Nov. 24, 1858.*

I have enjoyed several opportunities of visiting a very remarkable collection of paintings in the possession of Mr. James J. Jarves, — a gentleman who, you probably know, has been for several years a resident of Florence. From the commencement of his life in Italy, Mr. Jarves has been an earnest, thoughtful art-student. Starting with a great natural love for art, and a quick perception of the true manifestations of genius in it, he has become, by study and observation, quite a discriminating and learned connoisseur. He gave to the world some fruit of his study and reflection in his book, ' Art-Hints,' — a work which filled a vacant place in art-literature, and which cannot be too highly recommended to American readers on that subject.

Less than a year ago, Mr. Jarves began to put in execution a plan which he had conceived, of forming a collection of pictures which should illustrate the gradual progress made in the

art of painting, from the Byzantine style to that of the *cinque
cento*, and inclusive of both, — a period of five centuries, the
golden age of Christian art.   He has devoted himself to this
object with unwearied diligence, has neglected no opportunities,
and left no means untried for the accomplishment of his purpose.
He was fortunate in so far interesting in his object a friend and
lover of art in America, that funds sufficient to carry out his
plan were placed in his hands.   And his labors, thus far, have
been rewarded with a wonderful amount of success.   The collection already numbers about one hundred pictures.   Among
them are several pictures of the tenth and eleventh centuries,
and works of Margaritone, Cimabue, Giotto, Giottino, Masaccio,
Orcagna, Fra Angelico, Gentile da Fabriano, Fra Filippo, Botticelli, Ghirlandajo, Perugino, Fra Bartolommeo, Da Credi, and
Leonardo da Vinci.   He has been fortunate enough to obtain
several fine pictures of the interesting Sienese school; among
them two noble paintings by the great artist Sodoma, the rival
of Raphael.

Perhaps the gem of the collection is a picture by Leonardo
da Vinci.   It is one of the most perfect specimens of that great
master's peculiar management of light and shade, of his marvellous beauty of finish, and of his wonderful power in modelling.   The subject is a Madonna and Child.   The mother has
a face of great refinement, with sweet, delicate mouth and fine
eyes.   She sits holding the lovely child gracefully in her lap,
looking down upon it with an expression of the most exquisite
tenderness; forming, altogether, one of the most charming pictures that I have ever seen.

This collection is regarded, even by the Italians, as one of
the finest in private hands.   And if one considers the wide
range of art which it covers, and the great interest of the
period; the number, the variety, and the excellence of the
works comprised in it; and the opportunity it so easily affords
for studying the special merit and relative progress of so many
great painters, — I can hardly be charged with speaking too
strongly, when I say that it is only second in interest here to
the three great collections in the Uffizi, the Pitti, and the Aca-
demia di Belle Arti.   Its value, simply as a representative

gallery, can scarcely be too highly estimated. The collection has excited a great degree of enthusiasm among lovers of art in Florence, and seems likely to acquire very soon a European reputation.

Rio, the erudite author of "The Poetry of Christian Art," Mrs. Jameson, and Sir Charles Eastlake, are among the number of connoisseurs from abroad who have seen the collection, and manifested much interest in it. And the venerable and learned Cavaliere Migliarini, of the Uffizi Gallery, who is esteemed as the best-informed and most discriminating judge of art in Florence, has lately written a letter to Mr. Jarves, in which he expresses, in unqualified language, his admiration of the collection, and his confidence in the authenticity of the pictures. He considers that an extraordinary degree of good fortune has attended the efforts of Mr. Jarves; for, without such, no amount of pecuniary means, nor of knowledge, could have insured such great success.

---

## NOTE.

I have felt reluctant to print documents expressed in terms so flattering to my own labors, although kindly given for this purpose. Nothing short of the object in view could justify such apparent egotism. But, in laboring for a public object, the public have a right to call for the credentials of the self-elected laborer. Whatever confidence years of study and research may have given me in my own judgment, in this special pursuit, the public could not be expected to indorse it, unless, by a corresponding experience, it acquired similar knowledge. Failing that, it must rely upon the opinions of those qualified to speak. The necessity of putting before it such testimony, beside my own, is my apology for the prominence given to my own name. At the same time, I trust that I shall equally be pardoned in confessing that there is, in thus feeling constrained to fortify a position and aim that one *knows* to be genuine and useful, in order to obtain for them a candid welcome, a certain sense of humiliation which I would willingly have avoided. But now that my "old" friends are properly introduced to the public, with every desirable voucher for their worth, I trust the acquaintance will ripen to the benefit and enjoyment of all concerned.

JAMES J. JARVES.

New York, October, 1860.

MEMORANDA. — The paintings are numbered chiefly in chronological order. The numbers wanting on the walls belong to paintings not yet arrived from Europe.

ABBREVIATIONS. — *w.*, wood; *g.b.g.*, gold back-ground; *tem.*, tempera; *can.*, canvas; *enc.*, encaustic. Figures indicate the size in inches, in general including the frame.

For a full account of the Italian schools and masters represented in this collection, we refer the reader to " Art-Studies," a work on Italian Painting, in the course of publication by DERBY & JACKSON, New York.

# DESCRIPTIVE CATALOGUE.

1. BYZANTINE TRIPTICH. Artist unknown. (*Encaustic, g.b.g.* 19x9,) about A.D. 1200.

   Three compositions: right wing, the TRANSFIGURATION;* left, WANDERINGS OF THE ISRAELITES; middle part, DESCENT OF CHRIST INTO HADES.*

2. BYZANTINE. By the same hand. (*Encaustic, g. b.g.* 7x9.)
   The ANNUNCIATION.

3. BYZANTINE. By the same hand. (*Encaustic, g. b.g.* 7x9.)

   Representing the triumph of Christianity* over Paganism. Saints Dicaterina and Mercurios, whose names are given, are spearing the Roman Emperors, Julian the Apostate and Maxentius, from whose mouths issue flames. The Saviour, in the clouds above, is in the act of blessing the saints.

4. BYZANTINE. Artist unknown. (*Encaustic, w. g.b.g.* 6x7.)

   Style of the 11th and subsequent centuries of ordinary Byzantine painting. Represents the BIRTH OF THE SAVIOUR.

5. BYZANTINE. Artist unknown. (*Encaustic, w.g.b.g.* 14x13.)

   Represents the degenerate period of Byzantine art of the 13th and 14th centuries. MADONNA AND CHILD.

6. BYZANTINE. Artist unknown. (*Encaustic, w. g. b.g.* 5x6.)

   MADONNA AND CHILD. Degenerate period of Byzantine art.

7. BYZANTINE. Artist unknown. (*Encaustic, w. g. b.g.* 9x6.)

   A favorable specimen of the style of the 12th and 13th centuries. ST. GEORGE AND THE DRAGON. — "The legend of St. George came to us from the East; where, under various forms, — as Apollo and the Python, as Bellerophon and the Chimera, as Perseus and the Sea-monster, — we see perpetually recurring the mythic allegory by which was figured the conquest achieved by beneficent power over the tyranny of wickedness, and which reappears in Christian art in the legends of St. Michael and many saints. . . . The classical demi-god appears before us transformed into that doughty slayer of the dragon, and redresser of women's wrongs, — St. George." — Mrs. JAMESON: *Legendary Art*, vol. ii. p. 4. *Engraved Art-Studies*, plate C, fig. 11.

* Engraved and described. See " Art-Studies," chap. iv., plate A, fig. 1.

8. **Græco-Italian.**   Artist unknown.   (*Tempera, w. g. b.g.* 72x28,) A.D. 1190 to 1216.

An altar-piece. Two compositions, both mystical. The upper one represents the old and new dispensations, — CHRISTIAN BAPTISM by water, and JEWISH SACRIFICE by fire; the lower, CHRIST AND THE VIRGIN IN GLORY, surrounded by the angelic hosts of heaven. The MOTHER is doing homage to the SON, the conqueror of sin and death. Described and figured in Fumigalli's "Museo di Pittura e Scultura delle Gallerie d'Europa," Firenze, 1845, vol. xiii. p. 156. Do. "Art-Studies," chap. iv., plate B, fig. 4.

9. **Early Italian.**   Artist unknown.   (*Tempera, w. g. b.g.* 13x40.)   A style in vogue in the ninth and subsequent centuries, but not later than the thirteenth.

Three compositions: THE CRUCIFIXION; DESCENT FROM THE CROSS; ENTOMBMENT. An exceedingly rare specimen of the pure Italian art of this early period, and remarkable for the peculiar shape of the crosses (Y). Interesting for the architecture of that epoch, and as affording an idea of the starting-point whence originated the progress of the Tuscan schools that culminated in the greatest painters of Italy.

10. **Italian Triptych.**   Twelfth century.   (*Tem., w. g. b.g.* 24x15.)

Nineteen compositions: 1. The ANNUNCIATION; 2. BIRTH OF CHRIST; 3. ADORATION OF THE MAGI; 4. PRESENTATION IN THE TEMPLE; 5. BAPTISM; 6. ADORATION BY ANGELS; 7. LAST SUPPER; 8. AGONY IN THE GARDEN; 9. BETRAYAL; 10. TRIAL BEFORE PILATE; 11. JUDGMENT; 12. SCOURGING; 13. CRUCIFIXION; 14. DESCENT FROM THE CROSS; 15. BURIAL; 16. RESURRECTION; 17. ST. JOHN IN THE WILDERNESS; 18. MARTYRDOM; 19. HERODIAS. Before the invention of printing or engraving, this sort of painting was a pictorial Bible, as it were, for purposes of family instruction and devotion.

11. **Early Italian.**   A.D. 1200.   (*Tem., w. g. b.g.* 9x12.)

A TRIPTYCH of the debased mixed Italian and Byzantine styles, containing four compositions: the MADONNA, BAMBINO and two saints with angels above; the CRUCIFIXION, with the symbols of the eclipse; the ARCHANGEL MICHAEL trampling upon the dragon; TWO SAINTS.

12. **Giunta da Pisa.**   Painted from 1202 to 1253.   (*Tempera, canvas on wood, g. b.g.* 22x35.)

The CRUCIFIXION. Giunta has the dramatic energy of the Etruscan race, and marks the period when Italian art began to free itself from Byzantine domination, and create for itself independent schools of progress. This picture was designed for the upper part of a Gothic doorway, in a church near Siena. Engraved. See "Art-Studies," chap. iv., plate A, fig. 3.

13. **Margaritone of Arezzo.**   A.D. 1212–1290.   (*Tempera, g. b.g., canvas on wood.* 35x56.)

An altar-piece, of seven compositions. The central, the Madonna on a throne, sustained by angels, suckling the infant Jesus:

on either side, St. Peter and St. Leonard; the latter the patron saint of prisoners, slaves, and captives, — the Howard of his times. He died A.D. 546. Each wing contains three small pictures. 1st, Christ calling Peter. 2d, Fate of Simon Magus, who, undertaking, in the presence of the Emperor of Rome, to fly by the aid of demons, is dashed to pieces, in consequence of their being compelled, at the invocation of St. Peter, to let go their hold. A popular legend in the Middle Ages. 3d, Peter released by the angel from prison. 4th, Christ giving the keys to Peter. 5th, The Healing of the Cripple. 6th, Martyrdom of SS. Peter and Paul. Engraved. See " Art-Studies," chap. iv., plate A, fig. 2.

**14.** CIMABUE (Gualtieri Giovanni) OF FLORENCE. 1240–1302. (*Tempera, w. g. b.g.* 22x64.)

> MADONNA AND CHILD, SS. John the Baptist,* James, Peter, and Francis.

**15.** CAVALLINI (Pietro) OF ROME. 1259–1344. (*Tempera, w. g. b.g.* 48x40.)

> The ANNUNCIATION, — his favorite theme; broadly treated, after the manner of fresco-painting.

**16.** GIOTTO OF VESPIGNANO near FLORENCE. 1276–1336. (*Tempera, w. g. b.g.* 28x72.)

> A small altar-piece. The ENTOMBMENT; the Virgin and St. John, attended by angels, placing the dead Christ in a sarcophagus. Instead of blue, the Madonna is clad in purple, in token of mourning. Engraved. " Art-Studies," plate B, fig. 5.

**17.** By the same. (*Tempera, w. g. b.g.* 12x24.)

> The CRUCIFIXION. St. John and the Madonna weeping at the foot of the cross; the Almighty, in the clouds above, in the act of blessing. Beautifully treated; drapery and figures admirably designed, with great force and feeling.

**18.** SCHOOL OF GIOTTO. Probably, from its warmer tone of coloring, one of his scholars in the northern part of Italy. (*Tempera, w. g. b.g.* 52x65.)

> A magnificent TRIPTYCH, uncommon from its size and condition, with the arms of the noble VECCHIETTI Family of Florence, now extinct. In the centre is the MADONNA AND CHILD: the former in a rich Oriental garb; the latter partially undraped, and playing with a goldfinch, which, among the mystics, signified immortality, but, by the naturalistic artists, was introduced merely as a pleasing accessory. The upper portion of the doors contains the ANNUNCIATION; both figures being remarkable for tender sentiment and graceful attitude. Beneath, on one panel, is the CRUCIFIXION; on the other, a group of six saints, of both sexes, — probably the patron saints of the male and female branches of the family of the Vecchietti. Engraved. " Art-Studies," plate D, fig. 12.

---

* Engraved. See " Art-Studies," plate C, fig. 10.

19. CAPANNA (Puccio), FLORENCE, died 1334. (*Tempera, w. g. b. g.* 24x64.)

> A small altar-piece. DESCENT FROM THE CROSS.

20. By the same. (*Tempera, w. g. b. g.* 14x36.)

> THE TRINITY, with saints in adoration. A mystical, tabernacle-picture, for adoration in domestic chapels.

21. DUCCIO OF SIENA. 1290–1339. (*Tem., w. b. g. b.* 21x21.)

> A DIPTYCH, containing the CRUCIFIXION, with numerous figures of Roman soldiers, angels, and disciples; and the Madonna and Child, surrounded by adoring angels. See "Art-Studies," chap. iv., plate C, fig. 9.

22. SCHOOL OF GIOTTO. About 1350. (*Tempera, w. g. b. g.* 36x60.)

> An altar-piece. The MARRIAGE OF ST. CATHERINE.

23. SCHOOL OF TADDEO GADDI. A.D. 1350. (*Tem., w. g. b. g.* 24x30.)

> A TRIPTYCH, containing nine compositions, with the portraits of the family of the donors kneeling at the feet of the Virgin.

24. GADDI (Taddeo), FLORENCE. 1300–1352. (*Tempera, w. g. b. g.* 12x14.)

> SS. PAUL and PETER, from heaven, giving the Bible and sword to St. Dominic, who kneels to receive them. One of the saint's visions; only some authorities say it was a *staff*, not a sword, that was given. But Gaddi's sword is more in keeping with the founder of the Inquisition. Engraved. "Art-Studies," plate C, fig. 8.

25. By the same. (*Tempera, w. g. b. g.* 34x60.)

> SS. JAMES and JULIAN, and the ARCHANGEL MICHAEL. The "heroic" Michael symbolizes the final triumph of the spiritual over the animal in human nature. He is the captain of the heavenly host, and conqueror of hell. Gabriel announces to the Virgin her immaculate conception; Michael, her coming death. In this picture, the spiritual expression is well rendered, and its tones are clear and bright. It has also been attributed to Starnina of Florence, one of the Giotteschi, who flourished a little later than Gaddi.

26. GIACOMO DI CASENTINO. Died 1380. (*Tempera, w. g. b. g.* 14x28.)

> The legend of St. GIOVANNI GUALBERTO, founder of the monastery of Vallambrosa, in the eleventh century. Gualberto, although piously educated, was a dissipated noble; and having met, on Good Friday, the murderer of his brother, was about to kill him, when he relented, and forgave him, on his spreading his arms in the form of the cross, and reminding him, with piteous pleadings, of the sacred character of the day. They then both went to the Church of St. Miniato, where, upon their appearance together on amicable terms, the crucifix miraculously bowed its head towards them, in token of its approval. This is the moment the artist has chosen.

**27.** ORGAGNA (Andrea), FLORENCE, 1329–1389. (*Tempera, w. g. b. g.* 26x40.)

SS. AUGUSTINE and LUCIA. Two EVANGELISTS in the rondels above. St. Augustine carries the crosier and the book, denoting his office and position as one of the Latin Fathers. She bears the palm, the symbol of martyrdom. The lamp in her hand signifies divine light. From the Convent of San Salvi. Engraved. "Art-Studies," p. D, fig. 15.

**28.** By the same.

SS. DOMINIC and AGNES, with two EVANGELISTS. Companion-picture.

**29.** SCHOOL OF TADDEO GADDI. 1350. (*Tem., w.* 12x14.)

CHRIST'S AGONY in the Garden.

**30.** GADDI (Agnolo), FLORENCE. 1324–1390. (*Tem., w.* 11x12.)

ST. FRANCIS receiving the stigmata.

**31.** SPINELLO ARETINO (manner of). 1308–1400. (*Tempera, w. g. b. g.* 15x26.)

The CRUCIFIXION. Above is the pelican, — the emblem of redemption through Christ. Groups of disciples and Roman soldiery are curiously intermingled with saints and personages of other times, with books in their hands; St. Anthony, with his ubiquitous pig, being present. The figures, though long, are graceful, and the heads full of expression; the pallor of deathly grief being admirably rendered in the *fainting* women.

**32.** SCHOOL OF SPINELLO ARETINO. (*Tempera, w.* 12x24.)

Vision of Constantine, and the Fall of the Rebel Angels.

**33.** LORENZO DI BICI, FLORENCE. 1350–1427. (*Tempera, w.* 12x30.)

The miracle of SS. COSMO and DAMIAN, patron-saints of the Medici Family and of physicians. These charitable brothers were wont to administer medical or surgical aid to all who applied, without recompense, or respect of person. The legend reads, that a man in Rome, afflicted with an incurable cancer in his leg, called upon them for aid. They came to him while he slept, cut off his diseased limb, replaced it by that of a Moor who had just died and had been buried near by, and, anointing the new leg with celestial ointment, it became like the other. In the morning, the cripple, finding himself sound and well, recollected the vision; and, calling in his neighbors, they went together to the sepulchre of the Moor, and found that the cancerous leg had indeed been exchanged for a sound one. On the right is another miracle, in which they appear, accompanied by angels, saving a man who is upon the point of falling from his horse. This painting is probably an *ex-voto* offering to these saints for some supposed intervention on their part.

**34 & 35.** ORGAGNA (Andrea), FLORENCE. 1329–1389. (*Tem., w. g. b. g.* 15x37.)

ST. JOHN THE BAPTIST AND ST. PETER. Grand and stately figures, of high finish and perfect preservation. Specimens of the art of the Giotteschi, of equal condition and character, are exceedingly rare in any collection. Engraved. "Art-Studies," plate D, figs. 13 and 14.

**36.** SIMONE MARTINI (Memmi), SIENA.   1284–1344.   (*Tempera, w. g. b. g.*  13x58.)

The wing of an altar-piece, with a gradino containing the ANNUNCIATION. The main portion represents the story of the BIRTH OF THE SAVIOUR, — the appearance of the angels to the shepherds, the journey of the Magi, and the offerings at the manger. A fine specimen of this distinguished master, the drawing of the upper portion of which is preserved among the designs of the old masters in the Florentine Gallery. Engraved. "Art-Studies," plate E, fig. 17.

**37.** SCHOOL OF SIENA.   Dated 1370.   (*Tem., w. g. b. g.*  72x80.)

A monumental altar-piece, from the suppressed Convent of San Martini alle Selve, at Signa, near Florence. The MADONNA AND CHILD enthroned, with angels playing on musical instruments. SS. Albertus, Peter, Paul, and Anthony. Above, the Redeemer and the Annunciation. Broadly painted, after the manner of fresco. Dignified and impressive. Engraved. "Art-Studies," plate F, fig. 18.

**38.** GIOTTINO (Tommaso di Stefano), FLORENCE.   1292–1324. (*Tempera, w. g. b. g.*  18x38.)

A tabernacle picture. In the lower part, the MADONNA AND CHILD, surrounded by SS. JOHN THE BAPTIST, NICHOLAS DI BARRI, DOROTHEA, crowned with roses, and REPARATA, the virgin-martyr, beheaded under Decius when but twelve years old. She is crowned, and carries the palm with a cross upon a standard. From A.D. 680 to 1298, she was the patron-saint of Florence; and the Duomo was first dedicated to her. She rarely appears, except in early Florentine paintings. In the arch above is the Crucifixion, with its usual simplicity of treatment as a purely devotional composition.

**39.** By the same.   1292–1324.   (*Tempera, w. g. b. g.*  12x24.)

The BIRTH AND RESURRECTION OF CHRIST, in one composition. Origin and triumph of Christianity. A fine and characteristic specimen of Giottesque landscape. From the Rinucini Gallery. Engraved. "Art-Studies," plate C, fig. 7.

**40.** SIENESE SCHOOL.   About 1350.   A painting of similar technical character, in the Gallery of Siena, is attributed to AMBROGIO LAURATI.   (*Tempera, w. g. b. g.*  26x40.)

An altar-piece. The ASSUMPTION OF THE VIRGIN, or the union of the soul with the body. At the command of Christ, it has risen out of the sepulchre, and seated within the mystic nimbus, surrounded by an angelic host, is borne heavenward, amid hosannas, and songs of praise. This is one of the most poetical of the religious compositions, and rich in meaning. The Virgin is clad in white, to signify her victory over earth and its sorrows, and her elevation as the Queen of Heaven. Christ is seen above, with the divine crown which he has prepared for his mother, who is now to be united to him in eternal felicity and power. The coloring and ornaments, as, indeed, the treatment of the entire composition, have a spiritual significance, and admirably harmonize with the mystical motive of the artist. The rapt, ecstatic look of the Virgin is wholly of heaven; while her attitude expresses the intense fulness of her faith and devotion. In 1818, this painting was removed from an altar in the Oratorio dal Pedere Gazzaja, by permission of the Bishop of Arezzo, to the private chapel of the noble family in Siena who owned it, — a record of which is inscribed on its back. Engraved. "Art-Studies, plate B, fig. 6.

**41.** Fra Angelico (Giovanni of Fiesole, the "Beato"). 1387–1457. (*Tempera, w. g. b. g.* 24x54.)

The right wing of an altar-piece, from the suppressed Convent of the Salvi, at Florence: containing St. Zenobio, the patron-saint of the city; St. Francis, of Assisi; and St. Anthony, of Padua. St. Francis bears the marks of the miraculous stigmata; and the flaming heart in the hands of St. Anthony signifies fervent piety and love. St. Zenobio wears his bishop's robes. Although, as a composition, this does not give those qualities for which Fra Angelico is most remarkable, yet its execution, and the ecstatic expression of the saints, are strongly characteristic of the monk-artist.

**42.** By the same. (*Tempera, w.* 10x15.)

St. Christopher carrying the infant Christ across the river. This saint represents the principle of aid in difficulty, arising from a trust in Divine Providence; and is one of those Catholic apotheoses of the moral sentiments, colored by the traditions and superstitions of believing ages; just as St. George is the redresser of wrongs, the model of knighthood, the Christian Hercules.

**43.** Sano di Pietro, Siena. 1420–1462. (*Tem., w.* 12x60.)

The Gradino of an altar-piece, containing the story of the Kings of the East. Engraved and described. See "Art-Studies," chap. viii., plate G, fig. 21.

**44.** By the same. (*Tempera, w.* 52x32.)

An altar-piece, containing the Coronation of the Virgin, — the favorite subject of Sano, who is considered as the Fra Angelico of the Sienese school. Like the Assumption, this is one of the most beautiful and mystical compositions of religious art. It symbolizes the Church triumphant. The immaculate woman, in the purified tabernacle of her earthly body, clad in robes of celestial triumph, amid the melodies of the heavenly hosts, worshipped by a crowd of the redeemed, martyrs wearing their palms and crowns, virgins bearing their tokens of perfect chastity of soul and body, the pure lily, the great Fathers of the Church with their books, popes, bishops, monks, and men of all degrees, devoutly bows before her Son and God to receive the everlasting crown of her salvation, and recognition by the hierarchy of heaven as their divine mother and queen. Both specimens are in the best style of the master. Engraved. "Art-Studies," chap. viii., plate G, fig. 20.

**45.** Giovanni di Paolo, Siena. 1428–1462. (*Tem., w.* 8x12.)

The subject seems to be St. Catherine, of Siena, pleading before Pope Gregory XI. the cause of the Florentines. An excellent specimen of this interesting master, remarkable for his Paul Veronese tones of color and light and for the effective character of the heads. Engraved. "Art-Studies," plate F, fig. 19.)

**46. Sienese School.** About 1440. (*Tempera, w.* 12x18.)

St. Anthony tormented by demons. A popular legend of the Middle Ages.

**47. Sassetta, Siena.** Lived 1450. (*Tempera, w.* 12x15.)

St. Anthony tempted by the Devil in the shape of a woman. See "Art-Studies," chap. viii.

**48. School of Siena.** About 1430. (*Tempera, w.* 13x18.)

The Exorcising of Evil Spirits by the anchorites of the desert. The neophytes, purged of their inborn evils, in the shape of demons, are clothed anew in sanctified garments brought by angels, and join the ranks of the hermits.

**49. School of Siena.** 1450. (*Tempera, w.* 6x12.)

San Bernardino, the patron-saint of Siena, upheld by angels.

**50. Giovanni di Paolo (attributed), Siena.** 1428–1462. (*Tempera, w.* 8x16.)

A Martyrdom of a Bishop by a Roman Emperor. The simplicity of composition of this class of pictures at this epoch, the story being told by a few prominent facts, is in striking contrast with the academical and anatomical displays, and canvases crowded with details and accessories, having no reference to the motive of the picture, but introduced to exhibit the sleight-of-hand of the artist, which came into vogue a century later, when naturalism had fatally overpowered idealism and religious sentiment.

**51. School of Umbria.** Unknown. About 1425. (*Tempera, w.* 12x28.)

The Death of the Virgin. Christ and the disciples surround the death-bed. Some are reading from the Scriptures, while he has just received into his arms, unseen by them, the soul of his mother, in the form of a new-born babe. A beautiful conception of the early masters. This picture has been attributed to Buffalmano; but the richness of coloring, heavy, full folds of the drapery, and the entire sentiment, point to the antecedents of Perugino, in the romantic locality of Umbria.

**52. School of Umbria.** About 1490. (*Tempera, w.* 8x14.)

An ascetic painting, representing St. Jerome in the wilderness, and St. Francis receiving the stigmata. He is attended by his friend, the friar Leo, who is said to have been a witness of the appearance in the heavens of a seraph with six wings, between which was the form of a man crucified, whence darted streams of light that stamped his person with the wounds of Christ, — a miracle which took place after forty days' fasting in a cell on Mount Alverna, which is represented in this picture. Above, a miniature annunciation; and, below, a Piéta. On the back are the arms of the Medici Family.

**53. Neri di Bicci, Florence.** 1419–1486. (*Tem., w.* 10x10.)

The legend of S. Niccolo di Bari. The saint is throwing into the window of the house of a poor nobleman three purses of gold, which enable him to dower and marry his three daughters, and rescue them from a life of infamy. On account of the archaic character of this little painting, several critics attribute it to Cimabue, to whose figures these bear considerable resemblance in design.

**54. ANDREA DEL CASTAGNO, FLORENCE. 1403–1477. (w. 20x33.)**

ST. JEROME doing penance. The lion typifies solitude, and denotes his kindness to all animals.

**55. DELLO DELLI, FLORENCE. 1372–1421. (Tem., w. 26x72.)**

A CASONE, or front of a bridal-chest, used to contain the wardrobes of rich and noble brides. The spectacle is a joust in the piazza S. Croce, of Florence; and is highly interesting, as being a picturesque and correct view of the architecture, costumes, magistrates, nobility, and citizens of that city in 1400. The combatants are distinguished by their banners, devices, and arms. All the windows overlooking the scene are decorated with rich hangings; and the judges and notary, in their official robes, sit in the central ones, those on either side being filled with the beauties of the day. The coloring is brilliant, action animated and natural. The entire composition contains one hundred and forty-six figures; of which the boys, in their quaint costumes, full of juvenile mischief and curiosity, are not the least interesting. "Art-Studies," chap. ix.

**56. By the same. (Tempera, w. 8x13.)**

ST. MARTIN dividing his cloak with the beggar; representing a well-known legend of charity of the Catholic Church.

**57. PAOLO UCELLO, FLORENCE. 1389–1492. (Tem., w. 16x60.)**

STORIES from the ÆNEID. On the right, hunting-scenes, an agricultural country, forests, and distant sea-views, with shipping; in the upper part of the centre, the fall of Troy, and death of Hector; below, a marriage; on the left, the building of Carthage, with a curious display of building machines, &c. Farther on, the Tiber, Rome and its principal buildings, and a scene from Virgil. Seventy figures. "Art-Studies," chap. ix.

**58. By the same. (Tempera, w. 16x60.)**

Companion-picture, representing the VOYAGES OF ÆNEAS. Curious for its impersonifications of the gods, winds, &c.; its storms of hail, thunder, and lightning, excited by Juno and Vulcan, and appeased by Neptune; variety of vessels and galleys of that epoch, their peculiar management and rig,—the arms of the family who ordered the picture being painted on the sides of the ships; the comical displays of terror and energy of the sailors in the confusion of shipwreck; and, finally, their safe arrival into a fair haven and smiling country, where Æneas and Achates are welcomed by Venus.

**59. GENTILE DA FABRIANO (attributed to; his early manner). 1370–1450. (w. 19x60.)**

Casone, representing the "TRIUMPH OF LOVE." Forty-seven figures. From the gallery of the Prince Conti. The following is a translation from the Italian of a minute account of this interesting painting, ingeniously explaining the allegory:—

7

"It appears certain, that this lovely little picture should be attributed to Gentile da Fabriano; nor can it be better designated than by calling it the 'Triumph of Love,' as expressed by Virgil in his tenth Eclogue, —

' Omnia vincit Amor, et nos cedamus Amori.'

It may, in fact, be considered as divided into two parts, separated by a doorway leading from one into the other. In the left portion, facing the spectator, is seen a pavilion, under which three graceful figures are seated; and, on the steps of the pedestal, another equally graceful figure is kneeling, in the act of supplication. This one, and the middle one of the other three, have arrows in their breasts, which have been shot by a little Cupid hovering in the air. The supplicant is a youth in love with the damsel, equally enamoured with him, whom he demands from her parents. The satisfied expression and raised hand of one of them, as if to bless the union, testify that the desire of the lovers has been accorded. At the foot of the pavilion is a wood; and there, in an open space before the trees, the two spouses, preceded by a little white dog leaping with joy, — the assured symbol of unbroken fidelity, — commence a dance, in which the guests assembled at the marriage-feast join.

"Seated on the branches of a tree are two musicians, playing on the clarionet, zealously regulating the lively carols. All these figures are clad in tunics, over which are the long robes worn in the thirteenth century, which give majesty and decorum to the figures and to the entire scene. By this wood, through the aforesaid doorway, the kingdom of Love is entered. The spouses are introduced into it by two priests of the Deity; one of whom is surrounded by rays, and is perhaps more remarkable for beauty of mind than of body. Reposing in the air, between the summit of two mountains, — the dark representing sensuality; and the lighter color, chastity, — on a throne formed by two lions, on which he places his feet, seated on two black doves, is seen Love, with golden wings, a sceptre in his right hand, and a bow in his left. At the foot of the first mountain is Apollo chasing Daphne, who is in the act of being changed into a laurel; and on one side of the declivity of the same mountain are Venus and Mars, caught in Vulcan's net. Where the two mountains are united, in the plain by their respective bases rises, in the foreground, a beautiful fountain, throwing up its limpid waters to the throne of Love, and again falling in minute rain into an elegant basin, towards which Dante, Petrarch, and Boccaccio — who have sung so much and so well, in various ways, of this most captivating of human passions — are hastening on the left to quench their thirst. Dipping his right hand in the basin, and with the other shading himself from the rays of light, stands another figure, probably a painter, who, through the prism of the playful rain, is observing the marvellous effects of the same light divided into its seven colors.

"On the further side, other personages, of great distinction, are seen approaching the fountain, two of whom are crowned as sovereigns : and one, who is armed from head to foot, may possibly be Charlemagne, who, it is well known, often yielded to the shafts of Love; the other, a queen, — probably Semiramis, ' who legalized impurity in her kingdom,' — as though ashamed, turns her back on the spectators. These are followed by a warrior, also clad in iron, and crowned with laurel, leaning both his hands on the pommel of his sword, the point of which rests on the ground, as though to signify that he seeks repose from warlike fatigues in amorous delights. Behind them are crowded together other figures, to denote that they are all persons who are equally obedient to the dictates of Love, in one form or another.

"Lastly, in the background of the right-hand scene, appear the two spouses, escorted by the same priests, pierced both of them by the same arrow, to demonstrate that they obey one soul-affection of mutual fidelity. The bride is then matched over the mountain reserved for the chaste, as has been already stated, and conducted towards Love, in a chariot drawn by two stags with branching antlers, the symbol of eternity; and guided by the priest, in whom is observable the beauty of the soul, or of virtue, manifested by golden rays of light, and who is appointed to conduct true lovers to the happy kingdom of eternal Love. The forsaken husband, with uplifted arms, in vain attempts to follow her over the rugged pathway; and is therefore fain to turn his looks towards the chariot which bears away with it all his happiness, as though waiting for the moment to be re-united to her in a better world. This symbolizes the body, which, in the sepulchre, awaits the sound of the angelic trumpet to summon it to be re-united to the soul, which, transported to heaven, has abandoned it for a season on the earth.

"In this manner, the ancient masters of painting were accustomed to clothe their works in beautiful and moral conceits."

60. GENTILE DA FABRIANO (signed). 1370–1450. (w., oil, 34x45.)

MADONNA AND CHILD in a Gothic niche, around which are intwined roses and pomegranates. Gentile is the father of Venetian coloring, and this picture fully justifies his claim to the title.

61. Style of PIERO DELLA FRANCESCA, S. SEPOLCRO. 1398–1484. (Tempera, w. 26x70.)

Casone, representing the visit of the QUEEN OF SHEBA TO SOLOMON. Contains one hundred figures, and is exceedingly rich and varied in architecture and costumes, and its interblending of Oriental features with those of the day.

62. GOZZOLI (Benozzo), FLORENCE. 1424–1485. (Tempera, w. 42x42.)

The ANNUNCIATION. The Virgin is seated outside of a Florentine loggia, at the further end of which, through a door, is seen her bedroom. Her stately chair is covered with a golden cloth. Gabriel* appears, with golden slippers, and wings of great splendor. He is without the usual lily, and devoutly and reverentially folds his arms upon his breast, as he humbly bends before Mary to tell her of the glad tidings that are to come through her to earth. She listens to him with wonder and awe. The influence of Fra Angelico is seen in the spiritual faces of both ; but the treatment of the drapery, and modelling in general, show a decided superiority to Gozzoli's master. A very fine specimen of a rare and valued master.

63. MASOLINO DA PANICALE. About 1400–1440. (Tempera, w. 28x55.)

A tabernacle-picture, with the arms of the family who ordered it, representing the Madonna in adoration of the infant Jesus, in a varied landscape, in which appear SS. Jerome, John the Baptist, Francis, and Tobit and the Angel ; the Almighty above, with his hands through a cloud, blessing the scene.

64. MASACCIO (Maso da San Giovanni di Valdarno). 1402–1443. (Tempera, w. 13x18.)

Birth of ST. JOHN THE BAPTIST. One of the small pictures belonging to an altar-piece painted for the Carmine Church, at Pisa (Vasari, "Vita di Masaccio," vol. iii. p. 157). Although injured, it displays much beauty of composition, broad and masterly treatment of details, grace and dignity of movement, with great truthfulness. Engraved. "Art-Studies," plate H, fig. 22.

65. LIPPI (Fra Filippo), FLORENCE. 1412 ?–1469. (Tempera, w. 24x30.)

ST. JEROME doing penance in the wilderness (Vasari, "Vita di Lippi," vol. iv., p. 126). Formerly in the guarda-roba of the Duke

---

* Engraved. "Art-Studies," plate L, fig. 37.

Cosmo.  In fine condition.  The companion-picture to the St.
Augustine of the Uffizi.  Engraved.  "Art-Studies," pl. H, fig. 23.

**66.** FRA DIAMANTE, FLORENCE.  1450.  (*Tem., w.* 36x58.)

A tabernacle-painting, with family arms, &c.  The MADONNA IN
ADORATION.  St. Catherine and angels; background of flowers.

**67.** ROSSELLI (Cosimo), FLORENCE.  1416–1496.  (*Tempera,
w.* 28x60.)

The MADONNA IN GLORY, sustained by angels, with the lily in
one hand, and the infant Jesus in the other.  A mystical painting.
Engraved.  "Art-Studies," plate J, fig. 29.

**68.** PIERO DI COSIMO, FLORENCE.  1441–1524.  (*Tem., w.* 38x58.)

The story of ACTÆON changed to a stag by Diana, and devoured by
his own dogs.  It gives three points of time :  1st, His discovery of
the change by the reflection of his head in the water.  2d, His
horror and affright.  3d, Pursued and overtaken by the hounds,
urged on by the nymphs of the goddess, clad as huntsmen.  A
picture interesting for its landscape and animals.

**69.** By the same.  (*Tempera, oil,* 10x14.)

The three ARCHANGELS. — MICHAEL, GABRIEL, and RAPHAEL
the guardian, with Tobit; the donor kneeling in the corner.

**70.** SQUARCIONE (Franceso), PADUA.  1396–1474.  (*w.* 22x30.)

BIRTH OF THE SAVIOUR.  Above is seen the ALMIGHTY; a
grand figure, swooping down from heaven, amid a cloud of celestial
beings.  An angel is flying towards the shepherds.  Joseph and
Mary are bending in admiration over the miraculous babe.  Deep
and rich in color; finely executed, especially in the small figures;
and with a very solemn gradation of light, from the zenith to the
faint glow of reflected twilight in the far distance.  Some critics
ascribe this picture to Andrea Mantegna, when a pupil of Squarcione.

**71.** Unknown.  About 1470.  (*Tempera, w.* 20x32.)

A tabernacle.  St. VERONICA, with the miraculous likeness of
Christ impressed upon her handkerchief.  Appears to be of the
early German school.  Above, a Piéta, by another and inferior
hand, evidently Italian.

**72.** BOTTICELLI (Sandro), FLORENCE.  1437–1515.  (*Tempera, w.* 28x43.)

MADONNA AND CHILD.  Landscape background.  Jesus holds
the pomegranate, with the seeds displayed, — the emblem of hope.
The Virgin is the same tender, sad, sweet face that we see in his
Venus in the Uffizi.  Engraved.  "Art-Studies," plate J, fig. 30.

**73.** LIPPI (Fillipino), FLORENCE.  1460–1505. (*Tem., w.* 24x54.)

St. SEBASTIAN.  Background, a view of a part of Florence and
the neighboring hills.  The picture is dated 1479, — Lippi then
being but nineteen years old, — and is inscribed with the names of
those who ordered it.  Engraved.  "Art-Studies," plate H, fig. 24.

**74.** By the same.  (*Tempera, w.* 13x15.)

The DEAD CHRIST.  A devotional picture for a private altar,
which has suffered from the smoke of lamps kept constantly burning

before it, and the kisses of devotees. The face* is sweet and tender, and is the type of that of his best Madonnas.

**75. POLLAJUOLO (Antonio), FLORENCE. 1433–1498. (*Tempera, w.* 38x45.)**

HERCULES KILLING NESSUS for attempting the honor of Deïanira, the betrothed of Hercules, who had hired the centaur to carry her across the river Evander. Landscape, Val d'Arno, with the cities of Florence and Prato in the far distance. A fine picture of a very rare master. When obtained, the beautiful half-nude figure of Deïanira was entirely covered up; supposed to have been done in the time of Savonarola, from his objection to the display, in art, of female charms. Engraved. "Art-Studies," plate I, fig. 26.

**76. POLLAJUOLO (Piero), (attributed) FLORENCE. 1443–1496. (*Tempera, w.* 20x48.)**

A lunette. The ANNUNCIATION, with carefully designed architectural perspective and chiaroscuro figures, done with great freedom and precision. There is considerable to recall Giorgio di Francesco di Martini of Siena in this painting.

**77. VERROCCHIO (Andrea), manner of, FLORENCE. 1432–1488. (*w.* 30x45.)**

The BAPTISM OF CHRIST, in the "hard, crude" design Vasari ascribes to this master. This picture is varied considerably from his well-known masterpiece in the Florentine Academy, and, whether by him or one of his pupils, would seem to be of earlier date.

**78. MATTEO DA SIENA. Lived 1465. (*Oil, w.* 20x34.)**

MADONNA AND CHILD with angels; the rosary indicating that it was done for the Dominicans. It has the firmness, and precision of design, of Mantegna, — brilliant coloring, and much character in the heads.

**79. PINTURICCHIO (Siena), 1454–1513. (*Tempera, w.* 22x22.)**

A decorated waiter, on which bridal or natal gifts were sent. It was painted for the Piccolomini Family, whose arms are on the front and back. The subject is an allegory representing the "TRIUMPH of CHASTITY," taken from Petrarch.

**80. SIGNORELLI (Luca), CORTONA. 1441–1524. (*Tempera, w.* 20x24.)**

The ADORATION OF THE MAGI. A grand composition of twenty-three figures, which, although so small, have the breadth, largeness, and freedom of fresco. Formerly in the possession of the Archbishop of Cortona. A more perfect specimen in quality and condition of an early master, — this picture never having been varnished, or subjected to cleaning or restoration, — it would be difficult to match. It displays those grand qualities which made his works the especial study and delight of Michael Angelo. See "Art-Studies," chap. ix. plate I, fig. 27.

---

*Engraved. "Art-Studies," plate II, fig. 25.

**81. MANTEGNA (Andrea), PADUA. 1430–1506. (*Tempera, w.* 18x24.)**

The CRUCIFIXION. Figure of St. John, particularly noble, and with an intense expression of mingled devotion and grief.

**82. CREDI (Lorenzo di), FLORENCE. 1455–1531. (*w.* 12x16.)**

The ANNUNCIATION; dated 1508. In his most finished manner. Gabriel floats into the room on two little clouds. Engraved. "Art-Studies," plate L, fig. 36.

**83. By the same. (*w.* 11x13.)**

The CRUCIFIXION. Background, a beautiful landscape, filled with the solemn quietude of this master, with the story of the sepulchre; companion-picture to the above. Both were from a private chapel in the Borghese Palace, Florence.

**84. By the same. (*Tempera, can.* 30x55.)**

THE CREATION OF ADAM AND EVE. Quaint and curious. The latter composition, a repetition, is to be seen, in chiaroscuro, at the bottom of his "Annunciation," in the Uffizi.

**85. LORENZO DI CREDI. (Attributed) 1455–1531. (*Tempera, w.* 60x67.)**

An altar-piece, injured by an inundation of the Arno. MADONNA AND CHILD, enthroned; ST. SEBASTIAN, draped; and ST. JAMES, OF COMPOSTELLA.

**86. GHIRLANDAJO (Domenico), FLORENCE. 1450–1495. (*Tempera, w.* 14x24.)**

*Ex-voto* picture. MADONNA AND CHILD caressing St. John. Portrait of the donor on left hand; half-figure. Above, the Almighty blessing his Son. Background, a landscape, with his usual introduction of water. Engraved. "Art-Studies," plate J, fig. 31.

**87. By the same. (*Fresco on tile,* 21x24.)**

Portrait of a lady of the TORNABONI Family. Often introduced into his large frescoes, and reputed to have been his "ladye-love."

**88. COTIGNOLA (Girolamo), BOLOGNA. (*w.* 36x48.) 1475–1550.**

St. SEBASTIAN, crowned by angels. Cotignola was a scholar of Francesco Francia, and afterwards studied Raphael's manner. His style partakes of both of those masters. He is very rare and remarkable, as in this painting, for the wonderful sweetness of his heads, in which he is rarely excelled. The angels are full of grace, and remind one forcibly of the early manner of Raphael.

**89. FRA BARTOLOMEO, FLORENCE. 1468–1517. (*Oil, w.* 80x100.)**

An altar-piece. A Pietà. The dead Christ in the lap of the Virgin; the feet sustained by Mary Magdalen, the head by St. Dominic, whose features seem to be a likeness of Fra Angelico. The background, a broad and varied landscape; showing, in its horizon, changes of thought in the artist, with several scenes in the life of Christ subsequent to his crucifixion. See "Art-Studies," chap. xi.

**90. Albertinelli (Mariotto), Florence. 1470–1512. (*Oil, w.* 28x60.)**

An Angel; quite Venetian in color.

**91. By the same. (*Oil, w.* 28x33.)**

Virgin in the Egg. The mystic doctrine of the predestination of Mary; a recondite dogma, dating from the beginning of the sixteenth century. "The promise of the redemption of the human race, as it existed in the Sovereign Mind before the beginning of things."—Mrs. Jameson : *Legends of the Madonna*, p. 55.

**92. Raibolini (Francesco Francia), Bologna. 1450–1517. (*Oil, w.* 27x32.)**

Portrait of the Wife of Paolo (?) Vitelli, one of the tyrants or lords of Citta di Castello, in Umbria. The Vitelli Family exercised cruel authority over that city; but were finally insnared and murdered by Cæsar Borgia in 1502, and their possessions added to the Pontifical territory. See Machiavelli's "Relation of the Murder of Vitellozzo, Vitelli, Oliverotto," and other Roman lords, by the Duke Valentino.

The princess is in a rich costume, with an elegant head-dress; and is caressing a rabbit which she holds in her hands. The background is one of Francia's beautiful and characteristic landscapes, of great aërial transparency and clearness of tints, and is evidently a study of the scenery in the neighborhood of Citta di Castello. This valuable portrait of an artist rarer even than Raphael, whose early manner he so much resembles, with, however, warmer and richer tone of color, especially in the carnation of the flesh-tints, was obtained in 1839 from the Family Giovagnoli, to whom it came by inheritance from the Vitelli, now extinct. The high forehead and slightly defined eyebrows were the fashion among the ladies of this epoch, obtained by carefully removing the hairs from those parts of the head. Some of Raphael's Madonnas, especially the Cardellino, Gran Duca, and those of that time, possess the same characteristics, derived, no doubt, from his models, before his taste was wholly regulated by æsthetic rules. Engraved. "Art-Studies," plate M, fig. 38.

**93. Leonardo da Vinci, Florence. 1452–1519. (*Oil, w.* 22x27.)**

Madonna and Child. Distant landscape seen through open spaces in the architectural background of the principal figures. Engraved. "Art-Studies," chap. xiii., plate N, figs. 40, 41.

**94. Pietro Vannucci (Perugino), Citta della Pieve. 1446–1524. (*oil, w.* 21x27.)**

The Baptism of Christ. Above is the Eternal, in a circle of cherubim and seraphim; an angel on either side : below, John and Christ standing in a stream; Mary Magdalen on one side, and an angel on the other, kneeling; the landscape of a similar character to that of his great picture of the Entombment, in the Pitti. Engraved. "Art-Studies," plate K, fig. 32.

## 95. RAFFAELLO SANTI, or RAPHAEL SANZIO, URBINO. 1483– 1520. (*w.* 22x35.)

The MADONNA, ST. JOHN, and JOSEPH of ARIMATHEA, supporting the DEAD CHRIST, in a solemn, simple landscape, with a distant view of the hill of Calvary. The original design is by Perugino, and exists, in a fresco transferred to canvas, in the Albizzi Palace, Florence. Good judges have attributed this picture to Raphael, as being one of those he copied or imitated from Perugino when a mere boy in his studio. It bears the marks of the hardness and timidity of youth, with the pure ideal and religious sentiment that characterizes the earliest efforts of Raphael, when wholly under the influence of Umbrian feelings. The types of the heads are thoroughly Peruginesque, with Raphaelesque delicacy and refinement superadded, and recall several of his subsequent and more matured efforts. In several details of color and drawing, it is varied from Perugino's design, and in just those points indicating originality of thought and deeper purity of feeling, particularly in the treatment of the waist-cloth. In the fresco, Mary and John wear shoes, and the drapery nearly covers them: in this composition, the feet are naked, and the drapery is more open, showing them entirely. The foreshortening of the right knee of Christ is superior to that of the fresco: the Virgin's eyes are open, instead of being quite closed; and she holds in her hand her girdle, which has become loosened from her waist. In this picture, the shoulders of the Christ are heavier and harder than those of Perugino. The figures of St. John and the Virgin correspond perfectly with the same in the "Crucifixion," of Cardinal Fesch's gallery, now belonging to Lord Dudley, done when Raphael was but sixteen years old, in the manner of his master, but "surpassing him in intelligence of expression. The child-like beauty of St. John, and the deep, sacred grief of the Madonna, are given with indescribable intensity." — *Kugler*. The saint, in both pictures, wears the same closed tunic, with a similar pattern of gold embroidery on the breast, the fashion of which differs wholly from Perugino's. The Christ, in the latter picture, shows a great advance in drawing, both over Perugino and that of the Piéta, which is simply one of the many *replicas* he made of his master's pictures, with but very slight variations of treatment and design, and must have been done, judging from Lord Dudley's picture, when he was not more than fifteen years old. In excellent preservation, and taken from a villa of the Chigi Family, the great banker of which was the particular friend and patron of Raphael. If it be his, as we believe, it is his earliest known picture. Engraved. "Art-Studies," plate K, fig. 33.

## 96. LO SPAGNA (Giovanni Spagnuolo), SPOLETO.  Fld. 1500– 1530. (*Oil, w.* 20x31.)

MADONNA AND CHILD and St. John, between four saints. Lo Spagno's pictures are very rare. Next to Raphael, he was the best of Perugino's scholars, and excelled as a colorist. His Madonna is of the type of Perugino, with greater force and character, and equal sweetness. A foreboding of the sad destiny of the divine child in her lap colors her expression. The heads of the saints are worthy of the pencil of Raphael himself. The children are the least successful in design; while the coloring of the whole is so warm and harmonious as to have led good judges even, not acquainted with Lo Spagno, to attribute this picture to the Venetian school of the Bellini. Engraved. "Art-Studies," plate K, fig. 34.

**97.** VANNUCCHI (Andrea del Sarto), FLORENCE, 1488–1530. (*Fresco.* 30x40.)

MADONNA AND CHILD. A souvenir merely of this artist, showing his graceful design and coloring; the picture being almost destroyed in removing it from the wall to canvas.

**98.** By the same. (*Oil, w.* 56x72.)

Altar-piece. This picture has the cipher of Andrea, and appears to have been one of his early productions, or was done in his studio, by his pupils, under his inspection. It has suffered considerably, and was originally a votive offering in gratitude for delivery from some epidemic or plague. SANTA ANNA sustains the MADONNA AND CHILD on a throne. SS. ANTHONY and JEROME kneel in front; SS. SEBASTIAN and ROCH stand at the side; the background contains a view of the little town in the Mugello for which it was done.

**99.** Unknown. (*Oil, w.* 30x36.)

The dead Christ, sustained by Joseph of Arimathea. The design is by Andrea del Sarto, and his painting is lost. This picture comes close to him. If not his, by one of his best pupils; perhaps Puligo.

**100.** FRANCIABIGIO, FLORENCE. 1483–1524. (*Panel, oil.* 50x55.)

THE ADORATION OF THE MAGI. A crowded, varied composition, showing the great influence of Andrea del Sarto over his friend and fellow-artist.

**101.** BAZZI (Sodoma or Razzi), SIENA. 1474–1544. (*Oil, w.* 30x110.)

ECCE HOMO. A noble specimen of this rival of Raphael. The Wandering Jew insulting the Saviour as he bears his cross, attended by the guard, on his way to Calvary. The eyes of the Jew and soldiers have been revengefully scratched, as was the usual fate of those personages, in pictures, by the religious fanatics of the time. Engraved. "Art-Studies," plate L, fig. 35.

**102.** By the same. (*Oil, w.* 35x50.)

MADONNA, CHILD, and S. JOHN, with SS. BERNARDINO and CATHERINE, the patron-saints of Siena. His type of the Madonna, for womanly sweetness and grace, is equal, if not superior, to most of Raphael's.

**103.** PONTORMO, FLORENCE. 1493–1558. (*Oil, w.* 30x30.)

The MARTYRDOM OF THE THEBAN LEGION by the Emperor Maximin. One of the weaker efforts of this unequal artist. There is a repetition in the Pitti Gallery, stronger in color.

**104.** GHIRLANDAJO (Ridolfo), FLORENCE. 1485–1560. (*Oil, w.* 88x100.)

An altar-piece, painted for a charitable fraternity; taken from a suppressed convent. The MADONNA enthroned, with ST. JEROME

8

and St. Dominic. The star is in commemoration of the vision of his godmother, who saw one descend from heaven, and settle on his brow, when she held him at the font. The figure of St. Jerome is very Raphaelesque; and the landscape is full of varied and pleasing details, executed with much care, and delicacy of touch.

**105.** By the same. (*Oil, w. 26x36.*)

Two Angels singing.

**106.** Bellini (Giovanni), Venice. 1425–1516. (*Oil, w. 24x60.*)

St. Peter. Landscape background. A noble figure, with grand, flowing drapery, and rich in color.

**107.** Giorgione (Barbarelli), Venice. 1478–1511. (*Oil, w. 22x37.*)

The Circumcision. Exceedingly luminous and deep in color, with very noble figures, painted, as it were, with fused gems.

**108.** By the same. (*Oil, w. 30x26.*)

Portraits of André Gritti and his Sisters, about A.D. 1500. He wears the costume of a Venetian admiral, and was Doge from 1523 to 1538. Giorgione suffuses this group with his warm magnificence and aristocratic tone; the heads of the ladies being slightly idealized, while the features of the astute noble forcibly express his stern resoluteness and iron will.

**109.** Bellini (Giovanni), School of, Venice. (*Oil, w. 20x28.*)

Portrait of Cassandra Fedèle, of Venice, crowned with the poet's wreath. She was born in 1465; died in 1558. The most popular improvvisatrice of her day; possessing a rare genius for poetry, music, besides being learned in philosophy, theology, the classical languages, history, and literature. On great occasions, she was called upon to deliver public discourses in Latin before the Venetian Senate and the most distinguished persons of Italy. Venice, when she was invited by several of the contemporary sovereigns to take up her residence at their courts, passed a decree forbidding her to leave, "that the Republic be not deprived of one of its finest ornaments."

**110.** Basaïti (Marco), Venice. 1470–1520. (*Oil, w. 33x44.*)

The Virgin and Child; St. Magdalen offering a box of ointment; St. John. Beneath, two portraits, male and female, said to be members of the Sforza Family, *praying*, as was the custom in noble portraits of this time. Landscape background. Basaïti was a contemporary, and almost the rival, of Giovan Bellini. He is delicate and brilliant, with a firm touch, like the Flemish masters of his day, but avoiding their littleness of manner.

**111.** Domenico Becafumi (Mecherini), Siena. 1484–1549. (*Oil, w. 24x50.*)

St. Catherine Swooning; angels supporting her; Christ, attended by others, descending from heaven towards her. Landscape background.

**112, 113. By the same.** (*Tempera, can.* 30x60.)

STORIES from the LIFE OF MOSES, sketches of. Historical compositions in tempera, for the decorations of a church at Siena, in fresco. The Passage of the Red Sea and the Plague of the Fiery Serpents. These studies are admirably composed, telling the story at a glance, and show, in design, the influence of Michael Angelo.

**114. VENUSTI (Marcello), attributed; MANTUA. 1550.** (*Oil, w.* 20x24.)

HOLY FAMILY, after a design by Michael Angelo. "Venusti executed many works from his master's drawings, and is distinguished by a neat and delicate execution." — *Kugler.*

**115. VASARI (Georgio), AREZZO. 1512–1574.** (*Oil, w.* 40x44.)

THE DEATH OF LUCRETIA.

**116. Unknown. SCHOOL OF ANDREA DEL SARTO. About 1525.** (*Oil, w.* 28x40.)

PORTRAIT OF DANTE, taken from his cast.

**117. CESARE DA SESTO, MILAN. Fld. 1512.** (*Oil, w.* 30x40.)

PORTRAIT of a lady, in the style of Leonardo, presumed to be one of the beauties of the court of Ludovico Il Moro. Remarkable for its delicate yet masterly execution, and force of expression.

**118. CESARE DA SESTO (attributed to). Fld. 1512.** (*Oil, w.* 30x24.)

MADONNA AND CHILD, with the pink; landscape background, in the Roman manner. If not by him, by some scholar of Raphael.

**119. SEBASTIAN DEL PIOMBO (attributed to). 1485–1547.** (*Oil, w.* 26x34.)

This fine painting, interesting both as art and for the subject, is considered to be a PORTRAIT of VITTORIA COLONNA, done by the friend and pupil of Michael Angelo. It unites the warm, rich, grave tones of the Venetian school to the strength, and boldness of design, of that master.

**120. ANGELO ALLORI (Bronzino), FLORENCE, 1502–1571.** (*Oil, can.* 32x63.)

PORTRAIT of one of the PRINCESSES of the MEDICI.

**121. ANGELO ALLORI (Bronzino), FLORENCE. 1502–1571.** (*Can., oil.* 60x100.)

The ANNUNCIATION, a large altar-piece, in the weak coloring, but characteristic design, of the followers of Michael Angelo.

**122. PALMEZZANO (Marco), OF FORLI. Fld. 1513–1537.** (*Wood, oil.* 48x50.)

An altar-piece. ST. PETER, ST. PAUL, and ST. LEONARD; with the portrait of the donor kneeling. A school-artist of this period, of local distinction only.

123. PONTORMO, FLORENCE. 1493–1558. (*Oil, w.* 24x36.)

> PORTRAIT OF COSMO DE MEDICI, the first Grand Duke of Tuscany.

124. PARIS BORDONE (attributed), TREVISI, a pupil of Titian. 1513–1588. (*Oil, w.* 22x30.)

> PORTRAIT OF BIANCA CAPELLO.

125. Unknown. About 1530. (*Oil, w.* 24x33.)

> PORTRAIT OF FERNANDO CORTEZ, with the inscription, " Ferd. Cortez, Indor. Domitor."

126. ALTISSIMO (Cristofano), FLORENCE; a pupil of Pontormo. (*Oil, w.* 24x28.)

> PORTRAIT OF AMERIGO VESPUCCI in the costume of a magistrate of the Florentine Republic.

127. JACOPO DEL PONTE, scholar of Andrea del Sarto. (*Oil, w.* 24x30.)

> PORTRAIT OF PIERO STROZZI, Marshal of France, and son of Filippo Strozzi, the Tuscan Cato.

128. HOLBEIN (Hans), BASIL. 1498–1554. (*Oil, w.* 12x17.)

> PORTRAIT OF CHARLES V., Emperor of Germany.

129. Unknown. VENETIAN. (*Oil, can.* 28x33.)

> PORTRAIT OF POPE CLEMENT VIII.

130. GUIDO (Reni), BOLOGNA. 1575–1642. (*W., oil.* 9x12.)

> JOSEPH HOLDING THE INFANT JESUS; a "bozzo," or sketch from the Gerini Gallery, Florence.

131. DURER (Albert), attributed to, NUREMBURG. 1471–1528. (*W., oil.* 11x11, circular.)

> HEAD OF THE DEAD CHRIST, done with a painfully wonderful fidelity to nature, and thought to be modelled from his own likeness.

132. GERMAN. Unknown. Dated 1587. (*Oil, w.* 28x36.)

> The CRUCIFIXION, with a wonderful variety of detail and minute figures and architecture, illustrative of the painstaking littleness of many artists of this school.

133. BREUGHEL (Peter), the old German school. 1510–1570. (*Oil, w.* 20x23.)

> The PROCESSION TO CALVARY; curious for its spirited coarseness and movement, varied motives, and utter absence of the ideal or religious feeling of the Italian schools.

134. ZAMPIERI DOMENICO (Domenichino), BOLOGNA. 1581–1640. (*Oil, can.* 55x69.)

> Artemisia, a queen of Caria, who, in her excessive grief for the death of her husband, mixed his ashes with water, and drank them off. In Domenichino's best manner, and beautifully composed

in action and drapery, and with a face similar but superior to his Sibyl in the Capitol at Rome. Engraved. "Art-Studies," plate M, fig. 39.

**135. VELASQUEZ (Diego), SEVILLE. 1594–1660.** (*Oil, can.* 63x88.)

PORTRAIT OF A SPANISH GRANDEE, full-length; his early manner, harder in outline than his later, in the red-earthy preparation much used by him and Murillo. The armor is wonderfully metallic; "all sparkle and vivacity," as Wilkie describes it. The coloring rich and strong, and the touch bold and free. The greatest dark, and mass of the hair, is in front, the lighter gradation being carried *backward* instead of *forward*, which gives masterly relief to the head, and allows its contours to be lost in perspective, without any abruptness of outline; a treatment singularly effective. The background and outlines of the head bear marks of changes and obliterations in the progress of the painting.

**136. MURILLO (Estaban), SEVILLE. 1613–1682.** (*Oil, can.* 40x64.)

An Andalusian girl gathering fruit; landscape background. In female loveliness, Murillo was the Correggio of Spain. He diffuses a sensuous warmth over his pictures, unrivalled in that school: they are more poetical, with less force of individual character, than those of Velasquez. He painted young girls and children with particular delight; but was prevented by the rules of the Inquisition from giving the nude: hence the nearest approach he could make to it was in the decorous modesty of such a pose and management of drapery as this picture exhibits; enough to show his mastery over flesh tints, transparency of shadow, and graceful, light drapery, and hair, which seems literally stirred by the gentle breeze that is playing over the landscape. This profile, half-back view, with the drapery off one shoulder, is to be found in several of his paintings, —Eleazer and Rebecca at Madrid, the boy Christ and St. John at Munich, both in similar landscapes to this; though I know of none equal to it for sunny glow, and life-like qualities of flesh, fruit, and vegetation, with perfect grace of movement, freedom of design, and poetical warmth of coloring. See "Art-Hints," p. 281.

**137. CALIARI (Paolo), VERONESE. School of Venice. 1532–1588.** (*Oil, can.* 48x60.)

The CRUCIFIXION; treated with a solemnity of feeling and color rare in this master. It is the moment of the eclipse, when, as the heavens are darkened, Christ gives up the ghost. The good and evil physiognomies of the two thieves are forcibly contrasted. The Madonna has swooned; her girdle has been unloosed; and the group that sustain her, in the various emotions, and changes of hue in their complexions, as the harrowing spectacle of the dead Saviour is heightened by the intense agony of the mother, is admirably given. Its luminous management of the lights, and sparkle of color, exhibit some of the best points of this great master.

**138. By the same.** (*Oil, can.* 24x60.)

Christ in Glory, showing his wounds and cross. SS. Peter and Paul. A mystical composition.

**139.** RUBENS (Peter Paul), ANTWERP. 1577–1640. (*Oil, fine can., on wood.* 24x36.)

The CRUCIFIXION; treated in his usual forcible, naturalistic manner. Christ *hangs* by his arms, and we feel the painful tension of the limbs. A dog is knawing a bone at the foot of the cross. The Madonna and Magdalen are un-ideal, coarse women, vulgar and cold in their grief. There is no religious sentiment in the picture; but the horses, soldiers, the naked man holding up the sponge on a reed to the Saviour, the lurid gloom of the atmosphere, the sweeping, emphatic touch, and thin, lucid coloring, combine in this small picture the most prominent traits of this vigorous, courtly painter.

**140.** ROSA (Salvator), NAPLES. 1598–1641. (*Oil, can.* 56x44.)

LANDSCAPE, with figures fishing. Distant view of mountain, castle, lake, &c. The mid distance is singularly sunny and luminous. It has his monogram, — "S. R."

**141.** Unknown. BOLOGNESE SCHOOL. About 1650. (*Oil, can.* 40x60.)

MATER DOLOROSA; the Madonna holding in her hands the crown of thorns. The picture bears considerable likeness to the manner of Ludovico Carracci. See "Art-Hints," p. 358.

**142.** BOLOGNESE SCHOOL. About 1650. (*Can., oil.,* 38x44.)

MADONNA AND CHILD AND ST. JOHN. Several characteristics of Francesco Albani in this picture.

**143.** CARRACCI (Agostino), BOLOGNA. 1558–1601. (*Can., oil.* 46x60.)

VENAL LOVE. Cupid breaks his bow in indignation. A painting showing the influence of the Venetians, both in design and color, over the later Bolognese school. The grinning boy in the background has the face of the faun introduced by Annibale Carracci, in his masterpiece, in the Tribune of the Uffizi, — a nude Venus. From the gallery of Baron Von Bodenfeld, in Bohemia, where it was characterized as a Titian. Engraved. See "Le Peintre graveur par Adam Bartsch, vol. 18." — "Augustin Carrache, No. 114, p. 102," under the title of "Le Viellard et la Courtisane." The engraving is also by Agostino, and differs in a few unimportant details from the painting.

**144.** GERMAN LANDSCAPE. Seventeenth century. Unknown. (*Can., oil.* 55x65.) Style of the Boths.

**145.** GERARD (François), Baron, FRANCE. School of David. 1770–1837. (*Oil, can., oval.*)

PORTRAIT OF CHARLES X. in his royal robes. This portrait was a present from the king to his ambassador at Florence.

# WORKS OF JAMES J. JARVES,

PUBLISHED BY

HARPER & BROTHERS, New York; SAMPSON LOW, SON, & Co., London.

---

ART–HINTS : ARCHITECTURE, SCULPTURE, AND PAINTING. By JAMES JACKSON JARVES, author of "Parisian Sights and French Principles," "History of the Sandwich Islands," &c. Post 8vo. Cloth, $1.25; half-calf, $1.75.

"There are few subjects connected with art, in relation to its history, to matter, and to mind, which Mr. Jarves does not touch upon, and with so much freshness of thought, enthusiasm tempered with judgment, and sensibility to the beautiful, as to render his remarks no less pleasant to read than they are instructive. . . . His remarks evince sound discrimination and good taste. It is when we have such a book as this under our notice, that we find most occasion to regret our inability, from want of space, to quote from it." — *Art-Journal, London.*

"Fervent and useful, clever and well written. Mr. Jarves's language displays a strong nervous structure, that indicates a strong thinker." — "America has at last produced a writer who may help to educate her in art, guide her infant steps, and to point out the pitfalls that surround the pilgrim of art." — *London Athenæum.*

"This is the only way in which it is worth while to write about art; and Mr. Jarves, founding on high principles, and honest and acute in applying them, will be found, without at all rivalling such a man as Ruskin in depth or originality, well worth the hearing." — *London Spectator.*

" . . . We have seldom, indeed, read a book which excited more respect for the author, and sympathy for his opinions. His criticism is, in general, at once refined and elevated in spirit, animated by a thorough and patient knowledge of what he is describing, and, for the most part, singularly just and sound." — *London Guardian.*

"The work is one that may render good service to students in this country, as well as in America. It is a suggestive as well as instructive volume, and deals with the philosophy, as well as the facts, of the history of art." — *London Literary Gazette.*

"We commend the volume for its pleasant style, its varied historical facts, its fresh and honest criticisms, its rare good sense, its interesting analysis of art in different countries, its hopeful and healthy tone, and the importance of the theme to which it relates." — *Boston Transcript.*

"It does one good to fall in with such a book as this, — one that shows intimate knowledge of the subject it handles, and is yet free from pedantry or pretence; one in which the author's glowing enthusiasm is tempered by judgment and discretion. From its earnestness and loving tone, you might suppose it the work of a tyro; from its moderation, and respect for the opinion of others, it impresses you with the belief that the writer has pondered much ere he gave his opinions to the world. Not that he is deficient in boldness: very far from it. He sometimes runs counter to the general voice; and — what is a far better token of moral courage — he does not minister to national self-love." —*Albion, New York.*

"Gracefully and elegantly written, this work is destined to take rank with those masterly criticisms which have given the name of Ruskin such a world-wide reputation." — *New-York Herald.*

"Hardly a page of this book but abounds with thoughtful comment and valuable suggestion." — *New-York Churchman.*

" Next after Ruskin, we are disposed to rank the author of " Art-Hints." — *North-American Review.*

" Mr. Jarves has written upon a subject with which thought and taste, education and travel, enthusiasm and observation, have made him most familiar. He has written well, because with fulness of knowledge, and clearness of expression. At times, his language rises into eloquence; but it is always lucid, nervous, and harmonious." — *New-York Times.*

" Mr. Jarves's views on art are as remarkable for their calmness and good sense, as for their requisite appreciation of every form of genuine beauty." — *Courier and Enquirer, N.Y.*

" A work which every American tourist in Europe should read carefully before setting out, and consult frequently while among the art-collections of the Old World." — *Godey's Lady's Magazine.*

" A noble sermon on art." — *Christian Examiner.*

---

# PARISIAN SIGHTS AND FRENCH PRINCIPLES,

seen through AMERICAN SPECTACLES. First and Second Series. 12mo, with numerous illustrations. Price, $1.00 each.

" Terse and spirited." — *Blackwood.*

" A better picture of Paris, in so narrow a compass, we have never seen." — *N. Y. Courier and Enquirer.*

" As a shrewd observer, a stinging critic of society, and a lively narrator, we have not seen his superior for many a day. One of the most amusing books of the time." — *N. Y. Tribune.*

" Without question, one of the raciest books ever written upon Parisian life and manners." — *Boston Post.*

---

# ITALIAN SIGHTS AND PAPAL PRINCIPLES. With

numerous illustrations. 12mo. Muslin, $1.00.

" In variety of style, truth of description, and piquancy of criticism, Mr. Jarves has few competitors among tourists." — *New-York Independent.*

" Mr. Jarves combines many important qualities which are essential to the character of an intelligent tourist. He is evidently a person of education and refinement, conversant with the principles of art, as well as familiar with its chief productions; cherishing an interest in religious systems, apart from their external ceremonies; and accustomed to carry a critical spirit into his observations of nature and society. Hence the sketches of which this volume is composed are not only spirited, but informing. They furnish an impressive idea of the grandeur and the glory, and the degradation and shame, of modern Italy. They are not merely brilliantly colored pictures addressed to the eye, but pregnant illustrations of profound social truths. As a writer on art, Mr. Jarves will well sustain his reputation in this volume; while his description of ecclesiastical ceremonies, local scenery, and popular customs, will place him in the front rank of recent travellers." — *Home Journal.*

---

☞ HARPER AND BROTHERS will send either of the above works by mail, postage paid (for any distance in the United States under three thousand miles), on receipt of the price.